RISE
OF THE PROPHETIC
CHAMPIONS
Alignment Strategies for the Prophet & Apostle

Colette Toach

Rise of the Prophetic Champions

Author: Colette Toach
Graphics & Cover Design: Jessica Toach

ISBN-13: 978-1-62664-266-9

Other formats of this book:
eBook ISBN: 978-1-62664-267-6
Kindle ISBN: 978-1-62664-268-3
iBook ISBN: 978-1-62664-269-0

Copyright © 2023 by Apostolic Movement International, LLC
All rights reserved.

Published by Apostolic Movement International, LLC
5663 Balboa Ave #416,
San Diego,
California 92111,
United States of America

1st Printing September 2023

All rights reserved under International Copyright Law.
Contents may not be reproduced in whole or in part in any form without the express written consent of the publisher.

Unless otherwise specified, all Scripture references are taken from the New King James Version®. Copyright © 1982 by Thomas Nelson. Used by permission. All rights reserved.

While the author has made every effort to provide accurate Internet addresses at the time of publication, neither the publisher nor the author assumes any responsibility for errors or for changes that occur after publication.

CONTENTS

Preface 5

Introduction 7

PART 1: Alignment 11

    Chapter 1: The New Testament Alignment Model 13

    Chapter 2: Tribe. Clan. Corps Model 21

    Chapter 3: The Champion Model 27

    Chapter 4: Tribe vs. Corps 33

PART 2: The Champion's Sword 43

    Chapter 5: What Kind of Sword Do You Carry? 45

    Chapter 6: How the Champion's Sword Earns Its Name ... 53

    Chapter 7: Champions in Arms 59

    Chapter 8: Transition From Pastor to Apostle 67

    Chapter 9: The Killer Boy Band - Where Loyalties Lie 77

    Chapter 10: The Champion Killer 85

    Chapter 11: The Day You Earn Your Code Name 93

PART 3: Rank Formations 99

    Chapter 12: The Champion Who Lays Their Sword at Your Feet 101

    Chapter 13: Next Up: Champion Boot Camp 107

    Chapter 14: SOS: Submission 115

Chapter 15: SOS: Observance 123

Chapter 16: SOS: Service 131

Chapter 17: Arrange Your Champions in Rank and File . 139

Chapter 18: Coach. Position. Impart 147

About the Author... 154

Recommendations by the Author................................... 156

References and Citations 160

PREFACE

We live in both glorious and perilous times. We see bible prophecy fulfilled before our very eyes as the world plunges into a vast cavern of moral and spiritual darkness. At the same time, there is a radical outpouring of the fire and glory of God.

The question becomes, "Who will rise in this time?" Who will lead the next great move of God? Who will stand against the rampant moral decay and unashamedly declare the glorious gospel? I believe God is raising up a generation who will answer the call, and you are a part of that company.

There is a much-needed group of prophetic champions arising! They discern the call of the hour and the abundant opportunity for God's glory to invade the darkest spaces. These embrace the reformation prevalent in today's church. They embrace a church that is becoming kingdom-minded and moving behind man-made limits.

At the forefront of this movement is the awareness of the need for apostolic and prophetic partnership. The apostolic anointing is a trailblazing anointing. It receives marching orders and steps out to fulfill the will of God against all odds. Apostles are bold, rugged, and wired for radical obedience. They don't live in the world of popularity, political correctness, or human thinking. They are administrators of God's plans in the earth. They are spiritual architects armed with heavenly revelation and assignments.

1 Corinthians 4:1 Let a man so account of us, as of the ministers of Christ, and stewards of the mysteries of God. (KJV).

Paul stated that apostles are stewards (managers) of the mysteries of God. The apostle is given divine mysteries to manage in the earth in order to fully mature and equip the people of God. Each apostle has insight that's intended to accelerate their assignment in the earth.

Likewise, the prophet unveils the mysteries of the Kingdom and the testimony of the King. In Revelations 19:10, we're told that the spirit of prophecy is the testimony of Jesus. Prophets are accustomed to the realm of heavenly mysteries that point a dying world to the risen Christ. The prophetic voice is the one of repentance, intimacy, and radical love of Jesus. Prophets are the ones who cry against injustice and declare the will of God for people and places.

When the apostolic and prophetic align, there's unstoppable momentum. I believe this is a critical part of the next move of God. The reformers are linking up, not to further their name or agenda, but to boldly advance the Kingdom of God in the earth.

Apostle Colette Toach has been a trailblazing voice in the prophetic and apostolic movements. She has written many books that have equipped the ecclesia globally and impacted generations. In this writing, she manages to give us both prophetic insight as well as apostolic strategy to take our place as prophetic champions. This book is critical reading for those who are serious about their prophetic calling in this hour. As you dive into these pages, grab your notebook, highlighter, and a great cup of coffee!
Get ready to be challenged, equipped, and enlightened. You are a champion in the making!

Ryan LeStrange
Founder ATLHub and Bestselling Author

INTRODUCTION

God sent Craig and me to Mexico on May 5, 1998. My father arrived a year earlier and started a small mailing list. We didn't have any financial security. God never promised us grandeur. He only said, "I want you to go. I've called you to the nations."

And so, we left our church, family, friends, and security to enter... the wilderness.

Not a single ministry door opened. The businessman supporting us stopped all our income. So, we went to prayer. We spent hours a day in prayer and intercession. We contended for the nations!

We had incredible experiences in the spiritual realm. The Holy Spirit kept showing us huge keys opening doors to the nations. We decreed and sang in tongues for hours a day.

Our little mailing list grew to a whopping fifty subscribers. My father was a programmer by trade, so he wrote all our online systems. The odd $20 a week from love gifts kept three families fed.

As the Holy Spirit taught us what prophets were meant to do, we began teaching others. We sent a message online to all the other prophets out there, "If you're a prophet... we got work to do!" And so, our first prophetic school was born in 1999. It was one of the first of its kind on the internet.

And that's how we began. Mentoring prophets in the wilderness. We healed their wounds. We learned to equip them. Our mailing list became a school. The school became our door to the nations. In 2002, Craig and I were invited to Switzerland to establish live training for the prophets in the region of Berne.

Our feet didn't stop. With three little girls in tow, God sent us to find His hidden prophets. Our online school grew and continued to connect us with everyone we met. We're still connected with prophets today that we reached back then.

We reached them in their caves. We ministered healing as they wept at Brook Cherith. In 2009, our son was born. My father appointed us to apostolic office. He then handed the full leadership of the work to Craig and me. Our construction in apostolic trenches began.

We established ministry centers in California, Mexico, Johannesburg, South Africa and Berne, Switzerland. God sent us prophetic champions from all over the world.

For the longest time our ministry involved hours of training, counseling, and deliverance. It wasn't unusual to get a knock on our bedroom door in the late hours. We were spiritual parents to a team of prophets in desperate need of identity.

Together we learned the power of alignment. Each of us had a place. As apostles, we set structure. God imparted supernatural patterns. We leaned on the prophet's sniper view and passion to build. It didn't occur to us that God was revealing a pattern for prophetic and apostolic alignment. We just burned to reveal the heartbeat of Jesus to His church!

We liked our cave of Adullam: small group gatherings, hubs centered around prayer, training, and worship. By then I had around 39 books published. We found our happy place.

Then 2020 happened. The prophetic movement shifted. A call came to prophets near and far, "It's time to come out of the wilderness! The church is ready for you now. Arm yourself! Build!"

Charisma Media approached us to begin a podcast channel on their network. The Next Gen Prophets podcast channel was born, and we met Dr. Steve Greene. He was the publisher of Charisma and a former Dean of Business for Oral Roberts University. We knew him as Doc – a marketplace apostle who took us under his wing and changed everything. He didn't sugar-coat it.

"Colette!" he would say, trying to muster as much patience as he could, "Get out of the weeds! God has such big things for you, but you must shift! You can't stay in the trenches forever."

The penny took a while to drop. It wasn't good enough to stay in the wilderness. We had to come out! We had to build.

It was time to assemble the prophetic champions! As an apostle, God had me set protocols for our mandate. I was the glue and each of the prophets a brick in God's house. We depended on God. We depended heavily on one another.

A metamorphosis took place and further international ministry doors swung open wide. Today we team up prophets and apostles across the globe.

WHY APOSTLES AND PROPHETS ARE READY

While ravens fed the prophets at Brook Cherith, the apostles were called to the burning bush on Sinai.

Now as we're called to build, God needs us to get the memo.

God's man for the hour is over. God's prophetic champions are on the rise.

Apostles and prophets are building side by side. Prophets and pastors are digging trenches to prepare for a harvest of souls (spearheaded by the evangelists). Teachers are called to sharpen their swords. Champions are on the rise from the wilderness; armed, dangerous, and ready.

They're ready for you, apostle. Do you have the courage to lead the charge?

Ponder your vision. No matter how grand you imagine it, I promise you can't picture what's about to happen with champions at your back.

Prophetic champions are at the ready. Trust me, they're in every denomination and nation.

Apostles, God challenges you to assemble and train prophetic champions.

Prophets, God calls you out of the wilderness, off the podium, and onto the battlefield.

When you're a tight unit, you're unstoppable.

HOW I CAN HELP

The nucleus of our spiritual DNA is family and apostolic team dynamics. We're spiritual parents to the prophets and team builders of the fivefold ministry.

I divided this book into three parts. The first introduces the subject, and I direct it to both prophet and apostle.

The second speaks to the prophetic champion.

The third speaks to the apostle.

I plan to take nearly three decades of training prophets and give you the shortcut. I qualify because I mistook fools for champions. I'm here to help you discern who is legit. I'll help you differentiate circles of leadership.

Together, we'll navigate the importance of testing and sorting. You'll learn what's required to call yourself a prophetic champion.

If you've navigated this alone to this point, then you're in a good place. You needn't muddle through anymore.

I've got the battle plans. All you need to do is take notes and apply the strategy to your mandate.

PART 1: ALIGNMENT

CHAPTER 1

THE NEW TESTAMENT ALIGNMENT MODEL

Today we cringe at the blatant witchcraft emerging in our culture.

Silas, however, wouldn't have raised an eyebrow to see a shrine on the street corner still smoking from a sacrifice.

Both he and Apostle Paul were born into a world quite familiar with death and paganism.

We had the opportunity to visit Augusta Raurica – Roman ruins in the city of Basel, Switzerland. [1] The small museum displayed hundreds of excavated vessels and unpublished stories.

One display was an amphora housing the body of a baby. In an era of poor hygiene, infant death was common. They buried their infants in clay pots and often, amphoras. Infants under the age of 1 weren't mourned.

Women worshipped frantically at the shrine of the goddess, Juno. Survival wasn't expected, it was a "gift from the gods." The average life expectancy was 35. The world was poised for the birth of a Savior!

In our modern age, we don't comprehend the impact the alliance of a prophet and apostle made to their generation. When Apostle Paul taught us to put on our armor, he warred against witchcraft at the highest level. When he told us that God came to give us life, he shifted an entire generation's perspective.

He didn't do it alone though. He needed champions to break ground with him.

In that museum, Craig and I learned a powerful, documented truth. From one era to the next, a dramatic cultural shift took place. Christianity was born and the death rate dropped. With a firm belief in hygiene and prayer, churches became more than places of worship. They became prayer hospitals! Mothers lost hope in their pagan gods and searched out the church for help. Those who pleaded to Juno now worshipped at the Throne.

This is the world the apostles of our faith revolutionized.

POWER DUO: APOSTLE AND PROPHET

Today, God calls on us again. We're to become the catalyst for a world that's fallen back into satan's snare of theft, strife, destruction, and fear.

This book is a reminder of the power of alliance. It's not only God's will for prophets and apostles to align, it's His answer to our cry for revival.

Alliance: *a formal agreement or treaty between two or more nations to cooperate for specific purposes.[2]*

Align: *to arrange in a straight line; adjust according to a line.[3]*

We aren't doing anything new. Apostle Paul and Silas blazed the trail for us. They established an alliance that birthed much of our church culture.

To complete their joint mandate, they needed alignment. To be in alignment means to arrange in a straight line. Not only should the apostle and prophet establish a treaty for a specific mandate, we also need to do it in order.

Each needs to know their place. That's what I'll help you find in the pages that follow. The apostle is required to arrange the troops into a straight line. The prophet is required to add his sword to the ranks.

So, if you're ready...

COMPLETE YOUR JERUSALEM ASSIGNMENT

Acts 15:22 Then it pleased the apostles and elders, with the whole church, to send chosen men of their own company to Antioch with Paul and Barnabas, namely, Judas who was also named Barsabas, and Silas, leading men among the brethren.

Silas was a big deal! The New Testament church was in its infancy. Looking from the outside, it feels at times like the apostles made it up as they went.

They didn't anticipate the inclusion of God's blessing to the Gentiles. The first Jewish converts were considered a branch of Judaism. When Peter brought the first "unclean" into the Kingdom, he really messed things up for the circumcised lot.

So, when God called a well-educated Pharisee turned mercenary to bring salvation to the Gentiles, many had questions.

Apostles Paul and Barnabas took a trip to Jerusalem. During a famous counsel of all apostles of repute, decisions were made. The kind of decisions that changed the landscape of Christianity. [4]

I try to imagine what I would do if I were Peter or James. What kind of person would I entrust one of the most famous letters of our movement to?

Only two came to mind. Men of the highest caliber. Silas and Judas. Prophets.

As prophets in our era come from the wilderness, I look at their antics in the church and ask myself, "Are you men and women of repute?"

Before a prophet emerges as a champion, he must qualify in the local church. Many are capable of prophecy, but are you a prophet of such reputation that you qualify to be sent?

Silas didn't emerge as a prophetic champion until his Jerusalem assignment was complete. Prophetic champions are those who've served for a time under a pastor in the local church.

MAKE THE TRANSITION INTO UNIVERSAL CHURCH

Acts 15:34 However, it seemed good to Silas to remain there.

Once Silas completed his Jerusalem assignment, he was ready for the universal church. How many traveling prophets do we suffer who've never known the hard work of local church trenches?

It's easy to pass out words that split a church when you've never had to bleed for one.

Let's make a distinction between those who prophesy and the prophetic champion.

Before Apostle Paul and Silas could create an alliance, Silas had to shift. He couldn't stay at home. In this verse, we see that Silas made an uncomfortable decision.

He stayed in Antioch. He didn't return to what was comfortable. Remember, he was a leader back home. Everyone knew his name. Instead, he gave up his platform in obedience to God. He had no idea what God had in store for him. Obedience meant more to him than a platform.

He left home, mentor, and a leadership position to be sent... into the unknown. During this transition, God will align the apostle and prophetic champion.

ALIGNMENT - MUTUAL AGREEMENT

Acts 15:39–41 Then the contention became so sharp that they parted from one another. And so Barnabas took Mark and sailed to Cyprus; but Paul chose Silas and departed, being commended by the brethren to the grace of God. And he went through Syria and Cilicia, strengthening the churches.

Silas waited. In the meantime, God began to arrange the circumstances for Apostle Paul. A fight broke out and there was a split. Notice something.

Barnabas took Mark. Paul chose Silas. Silas did his part. He obeyed God to stay. Paul did his part. He chose Silas to accompany him.

Although the alliance is mutual, the apostle makes the first move. The prophet cannot impose himself on the apostle. He can, however, allow God to position him and accept the offer.

THE PRISON ASSIGNMENT

Acts 16:25 But at midnight Paul and Silas were praying and singing hymns to God, and the prisoners were listening to them.

Imagine it! Picked out to accompany one of the most famous apostles of the time! I wonder if other prophets were jealous? Silas had it made. Everyone knew his name now.

Yeah... I'm sure any delusions of grandeur evaporated when the whipping began.

This is where alliance is tested. It's exciting to build! To travel with a world-renown apostle... incredible honor! Oh, the things you will do together for Jesus.

Yet it's when you're thrown into prison that a true alliance is tested. It's here where most champions make or break it. When your apostle is slaying his ten thousands, it's pretty neat to fly his banner high!

What about when he misses it? What about when he messes up? I imagine Silas sitting there in that prison cell with Paul thinking, "Really Apostle? Of all your grand revelations and out of body experiences... you didn't see this coming?!"

It's around this time that some "feel led to greener pastures."

However, it's when you push through together during the worst of times that your alliance is firmly established.

Silas made a choice. When Paul began to sing, he began to beatbox.

He drummed such a beat, the Father began to tap His foot. The prison shook and the captives were set free! [5]

Many want the grandeur of saving thousands, but not many are prepared to go through prison to do it.

I often say that it's only when a relationship survives its first conflict that true friendship is forged.

It's only when prophet and apostle both get whipped and live to tell the tale, that an alliance is established!

PERFECT ALIGNMENT

1 Thessalonians 1:1 Paul, Silvanus, and Timothy, to the church of the Thessalonians in God the Father and the Lord Jesus Christ: Grace to you and peace from God our Father and the Lord Jesus Christ.

AGREEMENT OF DOCTRINE

Nothing like a near death experience to get everyone on the same page. For the prophet and apostle to be aligned, they need to agree on doctrine.

Silas was so invested into Paul's mandate that they wrote a couple of epistles together. You couldn't tell the difference between their voices.

Are you a prophetic champion? Then you have the same voice as your apostle.

JOINED MANDATE AND PROMOTION

1 Thessalonians 2:6 Nor did we seek glory from men, either from you or from others, when we might have made demands as apostles of Christ.

Paul's vocabulary changed over time from "my grace" to "we thank God without ceasing!"

My mandate became "our" mandate. "My" suffering became "our" suffering. In the passage above, Apostle Paul declares Silas as an apostle. He no longer differentiates between "yours" and "mine."

Alignment was complete. These men of God established the New Testament church. They turned the world upside down!

We all want alignment. Are we prepared to pay the price though? For true alignment, everyone needs to accept their part to play.

It's for the apostle to establish troop formation. It's for prophets to bring their swords to the ranks.

Until we've established this corps in the Kingdom, we can't begin to build.

CHAPTER 2

TRIBE. CLAN. CORPS MODEL

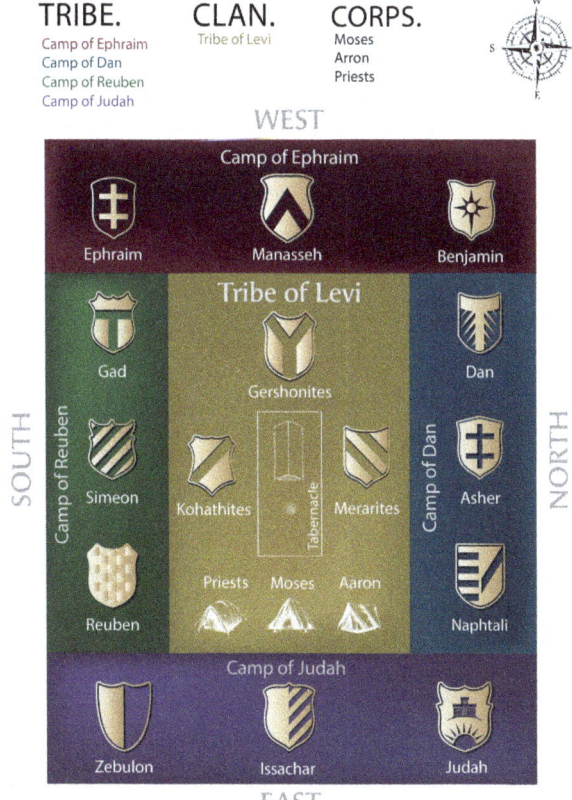

Figure 1: Campsite of Israel (Design by Jessica Toach, 2023)

Abraham was a wilderness wanderer. He birthed a family. Moses established a nation. A nation consists of tribes, clans, and the nucleus of them all is what I'll refer to as the corps.

Here is a drawing representation of the campsite of Israel after Moses built the tabernacle.

We see the ten tribes and the two half tribes camped by rank. Flanking three sides of the Tabernacle we see three clans: The Kohathites, Gershonites and Merarites. Each a collection of families from the tribe of Levi.

In this book, my focus is on the corps: The tents of Aaron, Moses and the priests.

We're well acquainted with tribes and clans in the Kingdom.

TRIBE

Genesis 49:28 All these are the twelve tribes of Israel, and this is what their father spoke to them. And he blessed them; he blessed each one according to his own blessing.

Now, apostles are natural patriarchs of Kingdom tribes. A tribe will share similar language, archetype, and spiritual grace. The tribe of Benjamin, for example, trained their men to fight left-handed to give them an advantage in battle.

APOSTLES ESTABLISH TRIBE AND CLANS

Every apostle has a spiritual DNA that's particular to their process. You'll see it within their tribe. However, within the tribe you'll find clans with a unique purpose.

Take the Korahite clan for example. They were from the tribe of Levi.

Their name might sound familiar. Their dad tried to stage a coup against Moses and Aaron (Num. 16:1-17).

Their grace wasn't to lead. God wasn't impressed and Korah ate dust. I imagine watching your dad and his buddies die by the hand of God would breed a healthy respect for the Father. History tells us that the surviving Korahites became worshippers.

They became gatekeepers, anointed with the gift of psalmody.

Their collection of psalms: Psalms 42-49, 84, 85, 87, 88.

Every clan has a purpose and we're grateful the Korahites found theirs!

And so, a tribe consists of a variety of clans. While clans share the same overreaching mandate of their tribe, their expression will differ from one to the next. There's a ton of space to express your individuality in an apostolic tribe!

A clan of intercessors can remain tucked in their prayer closet, while the clan of community workers ladle soup in the homeless shelter. We're all needed within a tribe.

To build the Kingdom effectively though, we need more than a tribe and clans. We need a corps. A team of champions to break ground. Without Joshua to win wars, Israel didn't have a safe place to camp.

CORPS COMES FIRST

Corps:
an organized subdivision of the military establishment
Marine Corps
Signal Corps

Synonyms:
Brotherhood, fellowship [6]

This is where we've missed it. Yes, apostles are called to establish tribe. However, when I study the lives of our patriarchs, I recognize that corps came before tribe.

Their corps broke ground for tribe. Their corps oversaw the multiplication of family and clan. It's the Kingdom way.

Apostle, if God's given you a mandate, you won't build it without a corps. They come first. Hence the rise of prophetic champions. God timed it perfectly!

Isaiah 60:4 "Lift up your eyes all around, and see: They all gather together, they come to you; ...

As the apostles are ready to build, the prophets are armed for war.

CORPS THROUGHOUT SCRIPTURE

MOSES

Exodus 4:27–28 And the Lord said to Aaron, "Go into the wilderness to meet Moses." So he went and met him on the mountain of God, and kissed him. So Moses told Aaron all the words of the Lord who had sent him, and all the signs which He had commanded him.

Moses' clandestine rendezvous with Aaron took place before they paid Pharaoh a visit. Moses had a mandate from God, but without Aaron, he wouldn't have made it.

We see the Lord add Miriam, Joshua, Hur, and Caleb to the corps. These champions saw the process through. When a couple of tribes wanted to hang back on the other side of the Jordan, Joshua made sure they fulfilled their promise to Moses (Num. 26:6).

When some clans tried to settle instead of fight, Caleb called the valiant to war to get the job done (Josh. 15).

The corps ensured the nation of Israel was established.

JESUS

John 2:1–2 On the third day there was a wedding in Cana of Galilee, and the mother of Jesus was there. Now both Jesus and His disciples were invited to the wedding.

Jesus' disciples had no clue how epic He was. If they thought He could teach well... I would've done anything to be a fly on the amphora when Jesus turned water into wine!

Some forget that Jesus gathered His disciples before they knew of His power.

Peter, James, and John were ready. In the same way, the prophetic champions are ready. They've been processed and they're itching to use their swords in battle.

DAVID AND HIS MIGHTY MEN

1 Samuel 22:2 And everyone who was in distress, everyone who was in debt, and everyone who was discontented gathered to him. So he became captain over them. And there were about four hundred men with him.

What a way to celebrate your call to the monarchy! Before David qualified to wear the crown, he assembled the champions in the back end of the wilderness.

His corps saw him to the throne. His corps saw Solomon succeed him. His corps worshipped at the dedication of the temple.

Apostle, you need more than a blueprint to drive your vision forward. You need a corps.

Recognize them. Train them. Release them to break ground.

This is the rise of prophetic champions and both apostles and prophets... are ready!

CHAPTER 3

THE CHAMPION MODEL

"If you want a job done properly, then do it yourself." Brave words of an idiot. That idiot being me.

It was 1999 and the launch of our first prophetic school. I was trainer, administrator, teacher, and workbook author.

The ministry took off and our school became an open door for church planting. My job titles reproduced like cats.

I was now elder, pastor, prophet, and counselor. Meetings, hour-long online chats, and non-stop calls made sure that everything was "done properly." So properly in fact, that I didn't see my kids one Christmas.

I was doing God's work. I was changing lives.

Question is... was I pursuing vision? If the enemy can't distract you from God's work, He will push you beyond what God intended.

Both attacks accomplish the same goal: to divert you from vision.

What sets this movement apart, is the rise of champions who drive the apostolic vision forward.

DAVID'S CORPS

As the Lord calls on His apostles to build, we need more than a team. We needed champions of valor.

2 Samuel 17:10 ...For all Israel knows that your father is a mighty man, and those who are with him are valiant men.

STRONG'S CONCORDANCE - "VALIANT/VALOR"

- ⇨ Strength
- ⇨ Might
- ⇨ Efficiency
- ⇨ Wealth
- ⇨ Army
- ⇨ Ability
- ⇨ Force [7]

These pages won't teach you how to staff your ministry with a team. It will teach you on the assembly of God's champions to create a corps.

INCREASE YOUR POTENCY

With the anointing God gave me, I could do some damage! Since then though, I've learned that a special forces unit can change the world.

Skill, talent, anointing, and authority can make a dent. However, will the vision of today's apostles maintain to the next generation?

One person can drive that vision forward to a degree. However, a corps of champions won't just maintain vision. They will push it beyond its capacity into mandate.

A CHAMPION STUDY

2 Samuel 23:18-19 Now Abishai the brother of Joab, the son of Zeruiah, was chief of another three. He lifted his spear against three hundred men, killed them, and won a name among these three. Was he not the most honored of three? Therefore, he became their captain. However, he did not attain to the first three.

Abishai had some swag. Who kills 300 men with a spear? No one I want to pick a fight with!

Even so, he wasn't the most famous of David's champions. Now, don't get me wrong, I think the strappy teenager who took down Goliath was pretty impressive. However, if you read through his list of champions, David pales in his metrics.

And that's why he was the greatest champion of them all.

David's valor didn't lie in his spear or sword but in his self-confidence.

It takes a man of tremendous gumption to surround himself with champions that could make him look bad. Saul couldn't do it.

David was stronger because he leaned on the strengths of his champions. It's a lesson you'd do well to learn from his example.

CHAMPIONS ARRIVE PROCESSED FOR SUCCESS

Reading David's champion list, I ask myself, "What kind of circumstance shapes a man to hurl his spear until 300 men lie dead?"

Eleazar fought until his muscles spasmed into a permanent sword grip. Yet, he continued to fight. Tell me, what does a man go through in his life to be at the point where he fights when he cannot fight anymore?

Yet, those circumstances created a man who paved a way for others to collect the plunder (2 Sam. 23:10).

In the same way, the prophetic champion is formed through pressure. You cannot create circumstances to impart the heart of a champion to any man. Only the Lord can set someone up with such tenacity.

The apostle's part is to recognize that potential. You can't shape a champion, but you certainly can draw out the diamond forged under pressure.

The apostle's part is to remain vigilant to identify the champions from members.

The apostle's part is to assemble the corps. The champion's part is to contribute their sword to the ranks.

CHAMPIONS ARRIVE PASSION-PACKED

I spent years trying to impart passion. I had a spiritual son whom I quickly deemed a champion. Sure, he hadn't killed 300 men with a spear nor busted through a troop to get me water, but he had a good heart.

He loved to give and was loyal. The hard part was his lack of passion for the work. So, I laid hands on him for impartation. I tried to hype him up.

I spent so much time trying to "passion him up" that the ministry suffered. He dropped the ball on every role in the ministry.

God told me to get out of the way. I did. Circumstances shifted until the Lord had him cornered. The Lord didn't give him passion. The Lord broke him.

Piece by piece, I saw the Lord crush his stubborn desires.

When he came to the end of himself, he shocked me. He found passion. He found his place. He flourished and... I had absolutely no part in any of it!

I learned many times that passion rests in the hand of the Father and in the champion He chooses.

When someone's ready to make the shift from tribe member to champion, they come passion-packed!

Apostle, if you're exhausted from trying to get everyone hyped, you mis stepped somewhere.

Your first mistake was assuming you're responsible for everyone's passion.

Your second mistake was appointing someone who didn't come passion-charged already.

You can give passion a direction. That's what Jesus did. Each of the Twelve were passionate.

James and John wanted to burn people to a crisp. Peter sliced and diced when he should've cleaved and sheathed. They had passion alright. Jesus directed that passion.

WHO GAVE YOU PASSION?

Why out of all your family are you passionate about the call? What makes you so different? Did your father or mother impart it to you?

Throughout history the greats were plucked from unassuming backgrounds. The passion you carry is a chromosome of your spiritual DNA. You cannot separate it from your identity.

In the same way we can't give someone blue eyes, we can't give someone spiritual passion. It's not our job.

I wonder as I write this, how much opposition you've faced over the years. How many times were you abused and rejected? Yet, here you are, driving the vision forward.

No man gave that to you. This DNA defines you.

Remember, Jesus didn't give His disciples a sales pitch to come on board. Peter, James, and John left their business immediately. Matthew gave up his career and his money.

Jesus kept it short and sweet, "Follow me." If you have to drum up someone's excitement for your ministry, they aren't a champion.

A champion ready to be assembled is equipped, processed and passion-packed.

CHAPTER 4

TRIBE VS. CORPS

2 Samuel 23:15–17 And David said with longing, "Oh, that someone would give me a drink of the water from the well of Bethlehem, which is by the gate!" So the three mighty men broke through the camp of the Philistines, drew water from the well of Bethlehem that was by the gate, and took it and brought it to David. Nevertheless he would not drink it, but poured it out to the Lord. And he said, "Far be it from me, O Lord, that I should do this! Is this not the blood of the men who went in jeopardy of their lives?" Therefore he would not drink it.

These things were done by the three mighty men.

David was the kind of man whose banner drew warriors everywhere he went. He boasted 600 members in his wilderness army. The three outlined in this passage weren't just members. They were part of the corps (2 Sam. 23).

David was very particular about who led his troops into battle. Every apostle should be this way. How do you identify a champion though?

Not everyone in the tribe qualifies for corps.

Like David, we want champions in the ranks that take the fight to the enemy.

Below are seven signs that separate a tribe member from a champion.

RISE OF THE PROPHETIC CHAMPIONS

1. MEMBERS RECEIVE. CHAMPIONS GIVE.

If you're a pastor, your members are your flock. My tribe are my Next Gen Prophets, disciples, and hub members.

We have a healthy agreement. They come to us to be fed. We feed them.

The member asks for deliverance and inner healing. The champion asks to learn how to heal and deliver others.

MEMBERS RECEIVE

John 6:30 Therefore they said to Him, "What sign will You perform then, that we may see it and believe You? What work will You do?

Jesus multiplied the loaves and fishes before their eyes. Not even twenty-four hours later and they wanted another sign. They wanted more bread. Don't be offended. Recognize the nature of a member. They came to be fed. So, multiply the loaves and the fishes to feed them!

CHAMPIONS GIVE

Mark 6:7 And He called the twelve to Himself, and began to send them out two by two, and gave them power over unclean spirits.

Jesus didn't entrust his authority to members. Only His champions. Champions don't want the bread so they might eat. They want the bread so they might feed others.

2. MEMBERS MINISTRY HOP. CHAMPIONS STAY THEIR GROUND

Listen closely! The Lord leads a member to receive ministry from various sources. They receive the element they need for their spiritual sustenance.

They don't occupy a seat in a ministry because they're sold out for the vision. They occupy it to get a need met.

When you always need, recognize that one ministry can't meet it all. If ministry is their desire, the Lord will lead them to sources to feed them. That often means reading books and attending conferences from all streams of ministry.

This is the nature of a member. Rest assured that at the end of their wanderings, a good member always comes home. No matter how many gadgets and goodies they find at a revival, there is still no place like the warm hearth an apostle has cultivated.

CHAMPIONS ARE LOYAL

A champion won't serve two apostles.

Many in Jesus' time flitted from one master to the next. Not the Twelve.

John 1:36–37 And looking at Jesus as He walked, he said, "Behold the Lamb of God!" The two disciples heard him speak, and they followed Jesus.

The two disciples spoken of here are Andrew and John. Not everyone left John the Baptist to follow Jesus. Some stayed faithful to the baptizer until his death.

The point is, champions are focused. Because their purpose is to give, they aren't torn between two leaders.

It's acceptable to expect your champions to be loyal to the apostolic vision. If they aren't, then recognize they're tribe, not corps.

3. MEMBERS TITHE. CHAMPIONS GIVE

Members can be a tremendous financial support to your ministry. However, not everyone who gives large sums to your ministry is a champion. I came to learn that members give for reasons that don't always feed my vision.

Firstly, they give to be in right standing with God. Remember, we need members in our ministries. They're the body's feet and Jesus needs them healthy and extending the Kingdom in their daily lives.

There are many who give, like the little boy with his loaves and his fish. They don't have the capacity to go into full-time ministry, but they can give what they have to make sure that you do.

CHAMPIONS SPEND PERSONAL FINANCES ON MINISTRY

Mark 10:28 Then Peter began to say to Him, "See, we have left all and followed You."

Craig and I love Caleb Wampler and Joshua Smith of *Kingdom Encounters International.* [8] They're next gen evangelists who lead hundreds of thousands to Christ each year.

Before their ministry became known, their funding bucket was pretty small. To get to India, they all had to dig deep into their pockets. It's a trend I've seen continue. As much as you can imagine their supporters sow into their ministry, you must see how much they and their team invest into it as well.

They didn't see their investment as paying bills. They're investing into vision for the reward of souls. Now that's a champion!

CHAMPIONS TAKE OWNERSHIP

We invest into what we own. When a champion invests finances into the vision, they change their vocabulary. They no longer say, "Your ministry. Their vision. My apostle's doctrine." They say, "My ministry. My vision. My doctrine!"

The apostles also paid that price to follow Jesus. Why? Because from the moment Jesus sent them out two by two, their membership shifted to ownership. This wasn't Jesus' vision anymore. It was theirs.

4. MEMBERS ARE GOOD CHRISTIANS. CHAMPIONS ARE GOOD EXAMPLES.

Every pastor wants a member who lives a godly life. I want everyone in my tribe to have a face-to-face relationship with Jesus. So, why did I make the mistake of putting undue pressure on everyone to be champions?

I expected everyone who walked through our doors to want to pay any price for the call. They were members. God hadn't asked them to pay that price.

He asked them to love Him. He didn't ask them to give up everything to follow Him. That's our job.

CHAMPIONS GO THE EXTRA MILE FOR JESUS

Matthew 26:40 Then He came to the disciples and found them sleeping, and said to Peter, "What! Could you not watch with Me one hour?

It's just as well Peter got a nap in before the big event. I point you to Jesus' tone here. He was exasperated with His disciples.

More is expected of a champion, and more is given. Pray longer. Fast more. Go without more. A champion gladly takes the lower seat and gives another the credit. Their flesh has often been called to Gethsemane and then Golgotha.

Because of this nature, a champion becomes a model for members to follow. Their life decisions and reactions to adversity set them up as examples, whether they liked it or not.

5. MEMBERS SERVE THE MINISTRY. CHAMPIONS SERVE THE VISION.

Romans 12:6 Having then gifts differing according to the grace that is given to us, let us use them: if prophecy, let us prophesy in proportion to our faith;

A healthy member flourishes in body ministries. They receive their gifts and gladly put them to use right away.

They're the ones who raise their hands when the call goes out to serve. "Please attend this Sunday and sign up if you'd like to serve in one of our ministries."

Pay attention. This is a healthy establishment of Kingdom purpose. Members should feel part of the tribe. They should connect with their clan! As we apostles drive the vision forward, members will flourish in the tribe we created for them.

CHAMPIONS MAKE THE TRANSITION

Champions are healthy members before they take to the battlefield. They serve until their hearts become loyal to the vision.

Apostles, don't expect loyalty to your vision if a champion never served. Until they've nurtured their grace in the basic work of God, they won't have your vision for the bigger picture.

A true champion has served in most departments and understands their place in driving the vision forward. This transition doesn't happen overnight.

They aren't hired mercenaries. They're nurtured members who rise from amongst the flock. They see beyond service times and hosting needs. They see the purpose of why these ministries are in place.

6. MEMBERS WAIT ON THE PROPHET, CHAMPIONS HEAR FOR THEMSELVES

Exodus 33:11 So the Lord spoke to Moses face to face, as a man speaks to his friend. And he would return to the camp, but his servant Joshua the son of Nun, a young man, did not depart from the tabernacle.

Joshua didn't wait to experience God through Moses. He remained in the tabernacle to hear God for himself.

When Moses imparted his authority to Joshua, he already knew where his power lay. Moses had no need to spoon-feed him. Israel was in good hands.

A member will seek out confirmation for the same decision from every prophet in town. A member will also believe every word a traveling prophet tells them.

A champion already heard from God and the prophet confirms their revelation. We need champions who can hear God clearly.

7. MEMBERS ARE HUNGRY SHEEP. CHAMPIONS ARE FEEDING SHEPHERDS.

A hungry member makes for a happy pastor. It doesn't make for a happy apostle though. Remember, we're speaking on prophetic, apostolic alignment here. When you lay an apostolic foundation, you don't need a needy team, you need an equipped team!

When Jesus fed the five thousand, notice this:

Matthew 14:20 So they all ate and were filled, and they took up twelve baskets full of the fragments that remained.

The disciples didn't come to Jesus with their hunger. They came to Him with the people's hunger. The disciples received a basket of bread each, after the party ended.

They were so caught up in organizing for the needs of the people that they forgot their own.

We should all seek God for more of His presence. Our hunger should match Joshua, remaining hours in His presence. A champion doesn't expect his apostle to feed that hunger.

A member does, though. They're sheep who follow the shepherd to better pastures. Members draw the anointing out of us. They make us better leaders.

Members inspire us to seek God for more to give.

A champion should link arms with you to serve the people, not remain a sheep who nips the heel of the shepherd for another snack.

ONE MORE CONFIRMATION THAT YOU'RE A PROPHETIC CHAMPION

There's one more characteristic that sets the champion apart from a member. God gives the prophetic champion a sword.

He's matured in all the body ministries. He's had encounters with all nine gifts of the Spirit. In fact, it felt at times like you walked multiple roads at once!

Over time though God thrust you into something. I'm reminded of Frank Hammond's testimony on how his deliverance ministry began.

He wrote, *"If you look outside on the ground, you will find furrows made by my toes when I was being dragged into this business. The Lord did not call me into this facet of ministry — He thrust me into it!"* (Hammond, 1990, p. 105) [9]

That's the prophetic champion down the line. God thrusts you in a direction and arms you with a sword to war. In the next couple of chapters, we'll focus our attention on that sword: what it is, what it does, and then... how to lay it at the apostle's feet.

PART 2:
THE CHAMPION'S SWORD

Prophet, your sword type is determined by its mandate.

Every prophetic champion comes furnished with a sword whose hilt fits snug in his hand. Not all swords are created equal, though. Your sword type depends on your process and purpose.

As we proceed, I'll help you recognize your God-given sword. We'll name it, and then I'll teach you how to put it at your apostle's feet.

CHAPTER 5

WHAT KIND OF SWORD DO YOU CARRY?

Zechariah 13:9 I will bring the one-third through the fire, will refine them as silver is refined, and test them as gold is tested. They will call on My name, and I will answer them. I will say, 'This is My people'; and each one will say, 'The LORD is my God.'"

Craig's office wall displays a collection of various swords and daggers.

So, when I come to the subject of the prophetic champion's sword, I have it on good authority that not every sword is created equal.

A samurai sword, the katana, takes a year to forge. Six months are spent on the blade itself and another six on the finishing touches. The process begins with fires of refining to turn iron-rich sand into chunks of iron.

Then, the beating and folding begins! After such an arduous process, only three of ten swords make the cut. Those that make it sell anywhere from $9000 - $2 million. [10]

The Samurais made famous the swords they carried. They were specialty weapons and belonged in the hands of highly skilled champions.

Rapiers on the other hand, don't take as long to make. They made the perfect personal sword because of how light and agile they were. They're just as deadly as the katana. You don't use it to slice a watermelon. It's perfect, one-handed use was for thrusting and jabbing.

Then, who doesn't love the broadsword? This commanding weapon did a good job at cutting asunder anything it pleased. It was difficult to master, but in the hand of a Victorian knight, it was a sight of terror. [11]

The sword you carry depends on your process. What we're looking for here is a mandate match.

Paul and Barnabas didn't make it as a team. Why? They had different mandates. Mark fitted best with Barnabas and Silas best with Paul.

Just as the apostle's gold has been refined through fire, so has your sword been forged in the furnace.

Your prophetic process prepared you for mandate. It's what sets you apart, champion!

A SWORD IS DEFINED BY HOW IT'S BEEN TESTED

Zechariah 13:9 defines the champion's sword. It smells like fire. A sword didn't have value on the blacksmith's bench. It only qualified once it tasted war.

The capacity for our anointing increases when we use what we have. When we face pressures beyond our ability, we grow. Where did you experience most of your pressure? Consider the ministries you served. Silas perfected his sword in Jerusalem way before he could offer it to Paul.

If a champion hasn't served under a pastor, they can't qualify to build with an apostle.

Champions have passed through fires of humility. They had to stand their ground when no one acknowledged their call.

A true champion doesn't drop their sword because someone doesn't believe in them. No, they get up and try again. Where did God keep asking you to use your sword? Look for environments that brought out the worst in you. The ones where you needed to go back and make things right.

The heat of the flame during your prophetic process defines your mandate.

Bottom line? Your sword smells like smoke.

WHAT ANOINTING IS IT ENDUED WITH?

Luke 24:49 "Behold, I send the Promise of My Father upon you; but tarry in the city of Jerusalem until you are endued with power from on high."

What anointing do you carry? This determines the edge of your sword.

Sword mastery takes time. Hours of training brings muscle memory into play during combat.

Anointing increases through battles won. For example, if you had to fight through sickness until healed, you're likely anointed to heal the sick. When you've battled demons, you become anointed for deliverance.

Because of the effort put in, the outcome speaks volumes.

A warrior who had to fight for the anointing on their lives is one who will continue to pay the price required for apostolic vision.

A champion is anointed. It's the anointing that makes for a solid alignment.

You're ready for alignment when you know who you are and what anointing you carry.

WHAT DOES YOUR SWORD DO BEST?

Every champion has a favorite gift of the Spirit. It's a unique spiritual DNA that took the Father years to forge in your life.

Look for a spiritual skill set that was proven over time. Silas was a prophetic leader with a ministry of exhortation. When you find the perfect blend of spiritual gifts and character processing, you recognize what you do best.

I work with a champion whose sword was forged for counseling. They function most in words of knowledge and wisdom. Another's was forged for spiritual warfare - his go-to is the gift of discerning of spirits.

God positioned you on many battlefields to test your mettle.

Every time you lost, you learned. Every time you won, you grew.

Your sword isn't new. You've fought to hold it!

Every champion has a blend of anointings and skill sets to bring to the table. To create a good alliance though, you need to know what you do best.

If the apostolic vision is for deliverance, then it stands to reason that a prophet with a strong emphasis on the gift of discerning of spirits would match.

Don't make the mistake of imposing your sword on an apostle who doesn't need it.

And apostle, don't just take on a champion because you like the look of their sword. Is it a mandate match?

Does it fit? Does the anointing align? Does the purpose align?

EVERY SWORD HAS A NATURAL ABILITY AND LIMITATION

1 Corinthians 13:12 For now we see in a mirror, dimly, but then face to face. Now I know in part, but then I shall know just as I also am known.

It takes a while for us to embrace our reality. A broadsword will dismember a limb but is most likely to lose against the quick jab of a rapier. Each sword has a strength and weakness. This speaks of the natural abilities God has given you. Recognize what you can and cannot do.

Your process exposed your flaws. It wasn't to break you. Rather, it was to recognize your limitation.

Okay, so you're terrible with people. But, I bet you're the kind of person who can war in the spirit until the paint peels. Stop being ashamed of what you cannot do and embrace your reality.

Rebekah, for example, is unable to make a final decision for anything. She chose her first dance wedding song a couple of hours before the ceremony. If I want quick decisions... hers isn't the sword I'm calling on!

Hers is a Katana; partly a weapon of war, partly a display of art. I can put her in the middle of any crowd, and she'll get on with anyone she meets. She is adept and precise at relationships. She doesn't like her limitation, but she has faced her reality. That's the power of being part of the corps. We have others who are better at decision making.

When you know the kind of sword you carry, you know where you fit in the ranks.

The maturity of a champion rests on whether they recognize their strengths and limitations.

THE CHAMPION RECEIVED A DIRECT INSTRUCTION FROM GOD

Silas didn't wait for Paul to decide for him. He made the decision to hang back at Antioch through personal revelation. Consider Moses and Aaron.

We get so caught up with Moses' burning bush experience that we forget to ask what happened to Aaron. God told

Moses that Aaron would meet him in the wilderness. This means while Moses had his encounter with fire, Aaron heard from God also.

He met with Moses along the way. Moses didn't need to send out a flare into the night.

In the same way, true prophetic champions can hear God for themselves. They don't require five confirmations before they go. As God arranges the apostle and prophet into perfect position, their aligned obedience ensures their paths cross.

To make the transition to champion, you need to hear God's voice very well for yourself. Look back over the assignments you've completed over the years.

God always positioned you. God gave you a job to do. You finished that job. Make a list of your completed assignments. What's the pattern? This pattern defines your sword!

If you know who you are and what God requires of you – you carry all the marks of a prophetic champion!

WHAT CALLS YOUR SWORD TO WAR?

John 18:11 So Jesus said to Peter, "Put your sword into the sheath. Shall I not drink the cup which My Father has given Me?"

Good ol' Peter. He was ready to throw down for Jesus. A champion is at the ready to defend his corps and apostle when the attackers come.

Many sing the apostle's praises when the bread and fishes are being handed out. You won't determine your loyalty in those times. You'll determine your loyalty when others speak behind their back.

You'll determine your loyalty when you jump to your apostle's defense publicly (without being asked).

Sure, Jesus had to say to Peter, "Put the sword away." It's better that way though. I'd rather tell a champion to stand down, then find him out of town when I'm being taken out by the hordes of hell.

So, champion, what calls you to war?

Other people can walk by the man beaten by the wayside, but the Samaritan picked him up. He felt the call to war.

Which areas cause you to leap to your apostle's defense? It's not something you pre-meditate. It's organic!

7. THE WEIGHT THE SWORD CARRIES

Mark 8:34 When He had called the people to Himself, with His disciples also, He said to them, "Whoever desires to come after Me, let him deny himself, and take up his cross, and follow Me.

Your sword is first proven in the fire. It's because your sword is tested that you carry the weight of the work with the apostle. If your sword was made for the battle, it will stand the test of time.

A champion who respects the apostle's fires of refining is one who bears the burden of the work with them. You make what's important to your apostle, important to you.

If the weight your apostle carries is in close quarters... your rapier can bear that weight. In battlefield warfare though, the apostle needs someone with a broadsword. My point is, what weights can you carry without flinching?

Jessica carries the weight of course creation with me. She makes it look easy. When Michael tried his hand at teaching, he jabbed when he should've blocked. He found the weight crushing! He spent weeks on his notes, and through much warfare, delivered it with passion but not a lot of principles. Jessica, on the other hand, easily sees teaching patterns.

Now, if there's a demon to slay... I'm calling Michael! He can stand in a room surrounded by demons and not flinch. What weight overwhelms others but feels easy for you?

WHAT'S YOUR SWORD?

During prayer one meeting, I had each in the corps seek God on the sword they had to bring. I said, "Ask the Holy Spirit to define the sword you carry. What does it look like? What can it do?"

Afterwards, they all testified of what God showed them in the Spirit. Chaifa received a simple broadsword. Rebekah's sword was ceremonial in nature. Michael's sword looked like a saber.

I said to them, "Recognize something. No two swords are alike! Your process, anointing, grace, and commitment sets you apart."

1 Chronicles 11:10 Now these were the heads of the mighty men whom David had, who strengthened themselves with him in his kingdom, with all Israel, to make him king, according to the word of the LORD concerning Israel.

Take a moment here to ask the Holy Spirit what your sword looks like. Can you see it? What does it do?

If you tracked with me through all seven criteria, then you aren't a member.

You aren't a spectator.

What you are, prophet... is a champion!

CHAPTER 6

HOW THE CHAMPION'S SWORD EARNS ITS NAME

In times past, it wasn't the beauty of a sword that determined its value. It gained value according to its performance in battle. In the Victorian age, swords were passed from father to son. Those who saw many battles held the most value. As times changed, swords of repute adorned castle walls used for pomp and ceremony.

HOW A SWORD EARNED ITS NAME

No one knew the quality of a blacksmith's work until the sword had been tested on the battlefield. Just the tiniest flaw and the blade would chip, or worse, break in the heat of battle.

Swords of ancient times were even imbued with human personalities and given names. When a champion went to war, the sword stood between his victory and defeat. The champion's grip of his sword told of his fear or anticipation for the fight. I can well imagine it a friend in the deadliest trenches.

After years of use, the sword had seen the champion at his strongest and weakest. It knew the taste of blood in the battle and the smell of earth after the rain.

2 Samuel 1:21-22 "O mountains of Gilboa, let there be no dew nor rain upon you, nor fields of offerings. For the shield of the mighty is cast away there! The shield of Saul, not anointed with oil. From the blood of the slain, from the fat of the mighty, the bow of Jonathan did not turn back, and the sword of Saul did not return empty.

The sword is mentioned often in Scripture. It's a weapon of destruction. It's a source of defense. Its blade told a story only known between sword and champion.

THE SWORD OF MERCY

When Craig and I visited the Tower of London, it was the day before the coronation of King Charles III. We booked the tour of the Crown Jewels. Instead of the Sword of Mercy on display, we got a note that read, "The Sword of Mercy was here..." as it waited in preparation for the next day's ceremony.

The Sword of Mercy has been used in the coronation of kings and queens since 1626. Once a sword used in battle, it now serves as a reminder of mercy.

Here's some of its story:

This famous weapon once belonged to Edward the Confessor (1003-1066). He was known as 'the Confessor' because of his deep piety.

The name Curtana comes from the Latin Curtus, meaning short. Interestingly the sword is also linked to some ancient legends.

According to one legend, the Curtana was the sword of Ogier the Dane, an 8th-century warrior. The sword bore the inscription "My name is Cortana, of the same steel and temper as Joyeuse and Durendal." It is said that Ogier drew the Sword of Mercy against Emperor Charlemagne's son in revenge for the murder of his son but stopped with a voice from Heaven called upon him to show mercy.

Today, the Sword of Mercy is on display with the other Crown Jewels in the Jewel House at the Tower of London. [12]

The Sword of Mercy isn't pretty. It's a short sword. Its broken tip tells a tale.

SO, WHAT'S THE NAME OF YOUR SWORD?

A champion's battle readiness is determined through their exploits on the battlefield. It's one thing to recognize your mandate, it's another to win battles.

What has God told you to do? Have you done it? A repeated obedience names your sword.

YOUR SWORD IS NAMED WHEN PUSHING THROUGH WEAKNESS

As believers, we face fire from heaven and from hell. A champion doesn't leave his sword in the dirt to escape the battle because he got bruised.

The Lord tests our mettle and satan tempts us to surrender. A champion navigates both.

What pushes you to your spiritual limit? Whatever puts your back against the wall time and again is a clue to your sword's name.

As we trained the prophets, I recognized that everyone has an "Achilles heel" that God addresses throughout their training. Do you remember the Greek story of Achilles? He was imbued with superhuman strength except in one area of his body: his heel. This weak spot led to his death.

In the same way, every prophet has a weakness that satan uses time and again to trip them up. Pride, family obligation, need for acceptance, fear of man, generational curses... it's a long list. What's yours? Helping the prophets recognize their weakness tipped them off to their spiritual strength!

1 Corinthians 1:26–27 For you see your calling, brethren, that not many wise according to the flesh, not many mighty, not many noble, are called. But God has chosen the foolish things of the world to put to shame the wise, and God has chosen the weak things of the world to put to shame the things which are mighty;

Weakness is where our battles are fought most. A champion is one that continues to fight battle after battle until the war is won. It's then you get to name your sword.

YOUR SWORD IS NAMED WHEN YOU COULD'VE QUIT, BUT DIDN'T

Not everyone navigates the pressure well. They come so far in their process and then hang their sword up for display. When you feel you've "paid enough of a price," your sword loses its edge in battle.

I've worked with more than one potential champion who quit before they were commissioned.

Just because you're called doesn't mean you're chosen. To qualify, you need to see the battle through. The Father is gracious. He always gives us second and third chances. However, let's return to the point of this book. This is *Rise of the Prophetic Champions.*

Not everyone with a prophetic call qualifies to build alongside an apostle. That's okay. Not every prophet is meant to. This book isn't written for the Sons of the Prophets (1 Kings 20 and 2 Kings 2).

Rather, it's written for the Samuels, Miriams, Nathans, Nehemiahs, Timothys and Silas'. These pages are penned for those who serve in the corps of kings and apostles.

1 Samuel 21:9 So the priest said, "The sword of Goliath the Philistine, whom you killed in the Valley of Elah, there it is, wrapped in a cloth behind the ephod. If you will take that, take it. For there is no other except that one here." And David said, "There is none like it; give it to me."

Before a champion can lay his sword at the apostle's feet, he needs to win his battle first. It took a point of no return before David picked up his sword. His was the sword of Goliath – owed to him from the spoils of the battle.

Yet, we find it wrapped up and hidden. When David had no choice but to escape and preserve his mandate, he picked up his sword. Not all prophets make that decision.

Prophet, if you dropped your sword because of need, hurt, and rejection, then it's time to decide if you're ready to follow through.

Satan tempts you to let it fall into the dust. A champion returns to his sword time and again for a fresh touch from God. We learn that our service to the King far outweighs any need for affirmation.

Our love for Jesus holds more value than the love of man. Our desperate hunger to please our Father feeds us more than recognition of man. A true prophetic champion knows whose Kingdom he fights for.

YOUR SWORD IS NAMED BY ITS METRICS

David's work began once he picked up Goliath's sword. He led an army of 600. He assembled his mighty men into a corps and established men of valor over them.

Your sword is named by the battles you've won. It's recognized by the ministries you've built and the divisions you led to victory.

So, what are your metrics in ministry? Make a list of your accomplishments, because in that, you'll find the name of your sword. You have metrics because you never quit!

My sword has changed its name several times throughout my journey. It began as trainer. It then evolved into scribe. Now, it's spiritual parent.

These aren't my callings. This is where my metrics lie. The name lies in the prophets I've trained, the books I've written, and the prophets I've re-parented.

The champion seeks the Kingdom first, whether all things are added or not. When you meet such a champion, you know. Their sword is battle worn. Their hands are strong. Their battle scars tell a story.

They carry the smell of smoke from refining fires.

Such is the nature of the prophetic champion and the grace of the sword he carries.

CHAPTER 7

CHAMPIONS IN ARMS

The men were outnumbered 12 to 1.
Israel: 3000 men
Philistines: 30 000 chariots and 6000 horsemen

It gets worse. Amongst those 3000 men, only two had swords – Saul and Jonathan (1 Sam. 13:22).

It's no wonder the Israelites ran from the battlefield. What they needed... was a champion! Jonathan was that champion.

While Saul offered the sacrifice out of panic, Jonathan made a plan (1 Sam. 13).

1 Samuel 14:6 Then Jonathan said to the young man who bore his armor, "Come, let us go over to the garrison of these uncircumcised; it may be that the Lord will work for us. For nothing restrains the Lord from saving by many or by few."

How many champions does it take to win a war? Two. Whoever Jonathan missed, his armor bearer killed.

They stirred panic throughout the camp. Once you recognize your sword's power, realize that its power lies in alignment with your peers.

This challenges your wilderness mentality. While you were in the dry lands, you adopted survival skills. None of these sustain you in the corps. You need another skill to battle alongside champions of repute. Some of them are stronger than you. Some will rub you the wrong way.

However, when you align with a spiritual kinsman, this happens:

1 Samuel 14:15 And there was trembling in the camp, in the field, and among all the people. The garrison and the raiders also trembled; and the earth quaked, so that it was a very great trembling.

Most imagine that the greatest challenge with apostolic alignment is agreement with the apostle. Not true. The real challenge is creating alignment with your peers.

In a champion corps, everyone arrives equipped. Your challenge is finding the slot for your sword. You'll only find its purpose when it joins the ranks.

1. GET HEALED AND DELIVERED

Proverbs 17:22 A merry heart does good, like medicine, but a broken spirit dries the bones.

Your wounds are breeding grounds for demons. The enemy wants to make you panic. Saul's rash decision to offer the sacrifice destroyed his alignment with Samuel.

His broken spirit lost him the kingdom. Inner healing isn't just a good idea for champions. It's necessary for mandate survival. You can't afford to bleed on the apostle and your peers.

The enemy knows your weakness. He's a dirty player. He won't come at you at first.

He'll allow you to join the corps. He'll even allow you to align with your apostle. And then, when you're needed most, he'll strike!

A heavy blow to your hidden wound will make you flinch. Then... he'll keep hitting until you're done. When your pain is exposed, satan will drive the knife deeper and twist it.

Offense manifests as bitterness. Rejection wounds grow to fear. Doubt becomes demonic conviction. Instead of decapitating the enemy, you drop your sword.

Your wounds whisper:

"It's happening just like the last time."
"They don't love you – they just want to use you to look good."
"They're manipulating you. You need to protect yourself!"
"Do you see how they spend money? Exactly the same way as the last ministry."
"They want to lord over you and waylay your mandate."
"They're more interested in building their empire than ministering to the weak and broken."

Except here's the catch: that wound is now home for a demon. Its voice continues to whisper until you break rank.

If you recognize a trend of failed ministry relationships, it's time to look at your wounds.

Just because you want to forget about them, doesn't mean the devil does. I've seen champions throw their sword into a ploughshare in the heat of battle because of manifested wounds.

It's not your apostle's responsibility to heal you. It's your job to seek out a pastor or fellow prophet. Get healed and delivered before signing up.

2. DITCH YOUR LONER MENTALITY FOR A CORPS MINDSET

Matthew 18:19 "Again I say to you that if two of you agree on earth concerning anything that they ask, it will be done for them by My Father in heaven.

There's no place for pride in a corps. You isolate because the devil lied to you. He told you that no one understands. He told you to wait until they prove themselves to you before you open your heart again.

Don't be tricked! The devil's playing on your pride. He puffs it up. Every time you place an expectation on someone to prove themselves to you before you'll offer your sword to them, you're bound by a spirit of pride.

Your eyes point inwards. That's not what Jonathan's armor bearer did.

1 Samuel 14:7 So his armorbearer said to him, "Do all that is in your heart. Go then; here I am with you, according to your heart."

He didn't force Jonathan to prove they would win before committing. He said, "I've got your back. Let's go!"

Self-isolation is pride manifested. Satan enthrones pride to hinder your mandate. He knows what happens when champions align. The ground shakes. Heads begin to roll. He'd rather keep his comfy throne on those strongholds.

Alignment doesn't just happen. It requires deliberate action. It means putting off your loner mentality and putting on a corps mindset.

SYMPTOMS YOU HAVE A LONER MENTALITY:

- ⇨ You never feel like you belong.
- ⇨ You feel corrected more than everyone else.
- ⇨ You mess up more than everyone else.
- ⇨ No one wants to hang out with you after ministry ends.
- ⇨ Look at the room. Everyone's sitting in a circle, and you're seated alone on the outskirts.
- ⇨ When you pluck up the courage to speak, no one listens.

If a number of these describe you, go back to the first point. Get healing and deliverance. Then follow up with action.

ACTIONS TO GET A CORPS MINDSET

- ⇨ Bind rejection thoughts. When you "feel" you don't belong, recognize the devil in it. Tell those thoughts to shut up.
- ⇨ Embrace correction with all joy. It makes you stronger.
- ⇨ Rejoice in your mistakes. Mistakes are opportunities for growth.
- ⇨ Don't wait for social invitations. Give them and arrange environments for social engagement.
- ⇨ Find a seat next to someone at the table.
- ⇨ Become a good listener and comment on what everyone else wants to talk about.
- ⇨ Don't apply these points once, twice, or three times. Make them a lifestyle!

To ditch your loner mentality for a corps mindset, perseverance is essential. This discipline takes months and sometimes years to master. So, get going. You got work to do, champion.

3. CELEBRATE WHAT WASN'T FAIR!

2 Corinthians 6:10 As sorrowful, yet always rejoicing; as poor, yet making many rich; as having nothing, and yet possessing all things.

Saul wasn't father of the year. The dude was ready to slit his son's throat for eating honey. Don't rule him out just yet though.

It's because of Saul's nature that Jonathan didn't fear battle. He didn't fear death. His father's ruthless nature played a part in his victory. The same holds true to your process.

Spend more time celebrating what you received than meditating on what past fathers did to you.

Your readiness to celebrate previous mentors, spiritual fathers, and pastors determines your qualification for corps. Apostle Paul gave us the shortcut in 2 Corinthians 6:10.

SORROWFUL, YET REJOICING

It's sad how things went down. You can't change the past. You can't heal what God separated. Allow yourself to grieve what happened. It's easier to be angry than hurt. Take time to hurt it through.

Then, rejoice in the fires that exposed your dross. Rejoice in the gold you mined throughout the process. Stack up the jewels you collected of knowledge, wisdom, and life experience.

POOR AND MAKING MANY RICH

You invested a lot! Money, time, and love. Become content with being poor. Your investment reproduces fruit in others.

The time and money you spent was not wasted. It shaped the sword you carry today.

HAVING NOTHING AND YET POSSESSING ALL THINGS

What do you call a millionaire who loses all his money overnight? Well... you call him a millionaire. His status isn't determined by how much is in the bank. It's defined by his ability to reproduce those millions.

Likewise, what do you call a champion who has been stripped of ministry, rank, position, and alignment? Well... you call him a champion. You're not defined by who recognizes you, champion.

You're defined by the sword you add to the ranks.

Next up, let's integrate you into the corps!

CHAPTER 8

TRANSITION FROM PASTOR TO APOSTLE

2 Samuel 23:15–16 And David said with longing, "Oh, that someone would give me a drink of the water from the well of Bethlehem, which is by the gate!" So the three mighty men broke through the camp of the Philistines, drew water from the well of Bethlehem that was by the gate, and took it and brought it to David. Nevertheless he would not drink it, but poured it out to the LORD.

Josheb-Basshebeth the Tachmonite (let's call him Josh), Eleazar, and Shammah were the mightiest of all David's men.

Josh could kill 800 men without help. However, when David craved a glass of water, he didn't attack the Philistine garrison alone. He roped the other two into his hair-brained scheme.

Their idiom was, "Friends don't let friends die alone."

How do you know if you're fully integrated into the corps? You're so connected to your peers that you blaze a trail. Your premise is, "It's better to ask for forgiveness than permission!"

FROM PASTOR TO APOSTLE

This requires a mindset shift. This chapter is perfect if you're making the transition from working with a pastor to an apostle.

Every champion served a pastor before they served an apostle. If you can't take the little skirmishes at the home front, you won't survive the onslaught in the trenches.

The three points below will help you make the transition. Josh and his buddies established David on the throne. They didn't prove themselves in David's fame. They proved themselves when they put their lives on the line for a drink of water.

1. MAKE WHAT'S IMPORTANT TO YOUR APOSTLE, IMPORTANT TO YOU

Josh got it. Water was important to David. So, they got David water. This act of loyalty moved David so deeply, he poured it out as a worship offering.

Here we are, thousands of years later, reading about their triumph.

For an apostle to lead the troops to war, he needs unity. A general can't lead a nation at war. When you pursue your own desires, you break rank.

Making what's important to your apostle, important to you doesn't negate your potential. It doesn't undermine your vision – it focuses it.

Can you boast the same metrics as Josh? He killed 800 and left a name for himself in history. This didn't come by pursuing his own agenda.

Rather, he pursued vision!

It's only when you function in a local church capacity that you get it. During your time serving your pastor, you see him flourish and fail. You see back-stabbings and renegades try to split loyalties.

The local church is your training ground. Prayerfully it teaches you that your vision is limited. It's easy to have opinions when the lives of the sheep are in someone else's hands.

A pastor has grace as you remind him of the new directions he should take. If he's a good pastor, he'll even encourage you to pursue your call. Pastors are equippers. They want healthy sheep to produce more sheep. So, if pursing your vision makes you healthy, he might support it.

When you can serve an imperfect pastor, you receive the character to align with a driven apostle.

God requires the apostle to design a blueprint. Building the temple was important to David. Bringing the tabernacle back was important to David.

When you align with your apostle, you celebrate the outcome. The mighty men got to see David on the throne. They experienced the glory of God as it descended upon the temple.

It won't always make sense. It might sound like, "that I could have a glass of water..." But this alignment changed the known world.

WHAT PRICE AREN'T YOU WILLING TO PAY?

I met a prophet who broke rank from a well-known apostle. She explained how her apostle had the desire to build a hub in her region; a launching pad of sorts for their international ministry.

She said, "But that's not what I'm here to do. I'm not here to simply build a launching pad for someone else when I have my own vision and call. So, I broke ties. No one will use me to build their platform."

This prophet gathered to her every other bitter prophet in the region. Together, they host meetings and speak often about how the renown apostles and prophets are out of order. This prophet won't experience the glory.

Glory of man, perhaps. She'll never experience the glory of God. So, what price aren't you willing to pay? She wasn't prepared to pay the price of alignment. She wasn't prepared to pay the price of making what was important to her apostle, important to her. Instead, she has the reputation of being a renegade and of questionable character.

APPLICATION:

1. What's important to your apostle for the ministry as a whole?
2. What's important to your apostle this month?
3. What's important to your apostle today?

2. PUT YOURSELF IN A POSITION OF SUBMISSION

Submission is a power move. When you're armed and dangerous and choose to lay down your sword, you show your worth.

If you've never submitted to a pastor, you won't cut it under an apostle. Submission to a pastor forges a "stickability" character in you.

A pastor will nurture the black sheep, whether he comes into line or not. If that sheep shows up for service, it will get fed. There's a little wiggle room in such a relationship. You can feign a headache and miss church.

You'll find less wiggle room with an apostle. If you missed an important meeting, they want to know why. Mostly they're thinking, "You didn't show up for battle when I needed your sword today. So, why should I call on you the next time the bugle sounds?"

1 Peter 5:5 Likewise you younger people, submit yourselves to your elders. Yes, all of you be submissive to one another, and be clothed with humility, for God resists the proud, but gives grace to the humble.

A leader shouldn't force you to submit. This Scripture says it plainly: choose to submit. Peter tells the younger to submit to the elders. Consider that the younger are stronger.

SUBMISSION TO YOUR APOSTLE

Peter calls on us to submit to those who are weaker and perhaps a little slower. Humility isn't speaking ill of yourself. Rather, it's the courage to choose to submit your strength to someone who's weak.

In the final chapters, I teach that apostles should expect their champions to have skills greater than their own. That's you! Of course, you're stronger and younger. That's not up for debate. But, are you strong enough to submit? Only you can answer that.

What does submission look like to you?

Blind obedience? Hardly. Submission is a choice to do things your apostle's way. It means to teach their doctrine. Invest into their vision.

If you have a different vision, then align with a different apostle.

Unity is a requirement for impact. Unity wins a battle. If you can't follow your commander in chief, you break ranks. The ministry loses. You lose. The Father will need to find someone else to win His war.

What will it take for you to do it someone else's way, in all joy?

The pastor gathers. The apostle sends.

SUBMISSION TO YOUR PEERS

Peter dives deeper. He says it isn't good enough to submit to the elders. He tells the church to submit to one another as well.

This level of peer submission between Josh and his buddies won wars.

Tough call! It's one thing to submit to someone you deem a spiritual parent. What about your peers? If your apostle chose well, you'll find many things to dislike in your peers.

I could tell you stories of how often Jessica and Dalton battled one another's flaws when they became corps. Dalton is the doer. Jessica is the thinker. She frustrated him with her seeming arrogance to do things right instead of quick.

He frustrated her with his seeming neglect of protocol and consideration.

After they hit heads for a while, he learned from Jessica to stop and read instructions before implementation.

Jessica learned from Dalton you'll never grow if you never have the courage to risk it all.

Now, just because they got it, doesn't mean they live in perfect humility. It's a daily decision to choose submission to one another. Don't think because you submitted "just this once," it's a done deal.

It's a daily protocol. Submit yourself daily to your apostle. Submit yourself daily to your peers.

When we submit ourselves to one another, Jesus Christ gets to lead and have His say.

THE POWER OF SUBMISSION

You invite Christ's power into your midst when you submit to one another. You fast, pray, and seek God daily for "more" when the solution is staring you in the face. Submission to one another brings Christ's power and the hosts of the heavenly realm to fight on your behalf.

Keep your rank. Respect your peers. Follow your apostle's orders, and together, you'll take ground.

3. LAY YOUR SWORD AT YOUR APOSTLE'S FEET

Pastors nurture. If you ask a question, they'll explain. Apostles... aren't pastors. Apostles are architects and builders.

Their investment is toward vision. A universal church vision! It's not in an apostle's vision to play church.

The pastor nurtures your skill set. The apostle leans on your skill set.

Approach your apostle with what you have to contribute towards the relationship. Pastors love health checks. Apostles look around the battlefield to see who's still standing and utilizes them in strategy.

If you get wounded... you're sent to the medical tent, where a team of pastors patch you up. Expecting an apostle to be a pastor is a huge dent to your relationship.

DAVID AIN'T YOUR DADDY

Remember, the champion's sword has been tried in the fire. Don't bring your sword and expect your apostle to forge it for you. Come with something to contribute. If you approach an apostle with a "you need to train me" mindset, you might find yourself at the back of the line.

David wasn't Josh's daddy. David was Josh's commander. I'm sure they swapped notes. They likely sparred in their spare time.

So, bring your sword and add it to the ranks. If your apostle has room for it, he will utilize it!

USE THE 4 POWER WORDS

Now, the apostle might not need your sword. He might require a secondary skill set that will take time to master. So, don't become embittered if you lay your sword at the apostle's feet and it's rejected.

Rather use these 4 power words, "How can I serve?"

APPLICATION:

What "sword" do you have to lay at your apostle's feet?

1. What ministry strengths do you have to contribute?
2. What natural strengths do you have to contribute?
3. From these two lists, which strengths does the apostle need?

CHAPTER 9

THE KILLER BOY BAND - WHERE LOYALTIES LIE

In ancient times, archers could sway the direction of battle. The only catch – they needed both hands to fight. They required a shield bearer to keep them safe as they took out their target.

Shields did more than protect. They expressed rank and culture. Their crest proclaimed their loyalties. Where do your loyalties lie, champion?

Loyalties are tested most when the killing begins. One doesn't know if a champion is up for the challenge until things get tough.

David's mighty men were tested.

1 Samuel 30:4–6 Then David and the people who were with him lifted up their voices and wept, until they had no more power to weep. And David's two wives, Ahinoam the Jezreelitess, and Abigail the widow of Nabal the Carmelite, had been taken captive. Now David was greatly distressed, for the people spoke of stoning him, because the soul of all the people was grieved, every man for his sons and his daughters. But David strengthened himself in the LORD his God.

David hit some hard times. Everything he fought so hard for... taken. Just like that, he went from Mr. Popularity to, "We wanna stone this guy!"

The champion pushes through such times. When the arrows begin to fly, the champion raises the shield. In that moment, the crest on his shield declares his loyalties.

The corps doesn't need you in the celebration. They need you when they've wept until they have no more power to weep!

Many years ago, we suffered a dramatic ministry split. In an instant, we lost finances, close relationships, access to resources, and direction for the future. I had to pick up the apostolic load. I didn't feel ready. I wept until I had no strength left to weep.

We had many prophets in our circle at the time. As Craig and I limped through the weeks that followed, there were some that lifted their shield to cover us. There were others whose loyalties to their own preservation became apparent.

Those who raised a shield covered our wounds. They prayed with us. Fought with us. They make the nucleus of our corps today.

Champion, your sword will win wars. Your shield will win the heart of your apostle and your peers.

THE KILLER BOY BAND

When David headed for Adullam, Saul gathered all the strong and mighty to himself. In fact, Israel wasn't short of strong and valiant men. They were a powerful army with many who could "slay their thousands." Saul was valiant and well known in battle.

So, what set David's champions apart? They were known as a band. They had one another's backs. They didn't pick out their individual strengths, but rather combined them into an immovable force.

When a champion won a battle, they all took it as a personal victory. David set the rule on this when half of his men took a city and the other half remained behind to take care of the baggage.

Upon their return, David said:

1 Samuel 30:24 For who will heed you in this matter? But as his part is who goes down to the battle, so shall his part be who stays by the supplies; they shall share alike.

In other words, they shared the glory. Whether they fought in battle or remained behind to take care of business, both were equally rewarded. Victory should be celebrated by all.

When you've waged war in bloody trenches, you're well aware that a victory isn't yours alone.

The commander cannot win the war without his champions. The champions are directionless without the bird's eye view of their commander.

A champion is quick to share his victories with his peers. When the praise comes and you're lifted up, lift up those who helped you get there. This will knit your heart to your team and your leader. Like David and his champions, you'll be a force to be reckoned with!

DEVELOP LATERAL RELATIONSHIPS

The relationships amongst David's champions outlasted his lifespan.

The love Jesus' disciples had for one another, survived his crucifixion and sustained them through persecution.

The Pharisees didn't get it. They just wanted to join the cool kids club with matching aprons and breastplates. Every relationship was a power play. They made a mistake with Jesus and His disciples. They figured if they got rid of Jesus, His disciples would scatter.

They didn't account for how Jesus established His champions. It wasn't just Jesus who drove the vision forward. The disciples did it together!

Lateral relationships will get you through the toughest times. Take time to develop a personal relationship with every person in the corps.

John 13:35 By this all will know that you are My disciples, if you have love for one another."

I've seen ministries split because of this lack. I've seen ministries where every champion tried so hard to impress their leader, they stepped on one another to be seen.

None of the disciples had to compete for Jesus' affection. He loved them all. More importantly, they loved one another.

Good relationships require investment. Make deliberate investments into each lateral relationship within your corps.

EVOLVE!

When God evolved our ministry into the Next Gen Prophets, I instantly noticed how many old gen we had hanging around.

They were easy to spot, and they couldn't make the shift with us. They liked doing things the old way. The prophetic move is well underway. What we saw twenty years ago has changed dramatically!

In 1999, we were reaching prophets in the wilderness, because many had been kicked out of their churches. Today, prophets have a place within the church. Many more leaders recognize their value.

When we shifted from hiding prophets in a cave to calling them to take their place, not everyone wanted to shift. They become comfortable in their hidey hole.

Don't be that guy.

When you get to the place of refusing to step forward, you say, "I refuse to surrender, Father." You tell God you want control instead of handing it over to Him.

How many lose out on the power of the Holy Spirit because they're afraid of how strange they might look? The day you refuse to take the next step alongside your peers, is the day you're left behind.

Either evolve or consider that your time with this apostle has come to an end. You can't remain in one place while God shifts. There comes a time when a battle is won, and a new battlefield awaits.

Ask yourself: Am I equipped for the next battlefield?

If so, then learn a new battle strategy.

Nothing stunts the growth of a ministry more than those who dig their heels in and refuse to evolve. Embrace the stretching of the new season.

Allow the Lord to challenge you in your place of weakness. Apostle Paul said he was all things to all men.[13] His growth had no limit.

When you allow the Holy Spirit to equip you, you'll receive a new anointing to go along with the next battlefield.

BURN YOUR ESCAPE ROUTE

You signed a political death warrant if you joined David in the cave. Once you crossed that line, you got a mention on Saul's hit list.

When Jesus called His disciples, He didn't call them for a temp job. He didn't say, "You're here for a season to get all my anointing. Then you can take everything I gave you and build an independent ministry."

I'm sure the Father considered many factors when He told Jesus to pick out the Twelve, but I see something they all had in common: They burned their bridges. They were all in.

Mark 10:28 Then Peter began to say to Him, "See, we have left all and followed You.

Where do you see yourself in another ten years? If it isn't worshipping at the dedication of Solomon's temple, you won't cut it.

Don't step over the threshold with one foot but keep a back door open just in case you want to run.

FEELING ALONE IN THE CROWD?

If you do that, you'll never feel like you belong. Do you feel like you don't have a place? Could it be that you have an "escape route" plotted in case things don't work out?

While you're still planning your escape, you never integrate. How many times have you thought, "Well, if this doesn't work out then…"

The Lord burned that bridge for me a long time ago. He refuses to allow me to think along these lines when He drops another champion at my door. I cannot afford to say, "Well, if they leave then…" No, I see them as part of my future.

Does it hurt when some let me down? Of course, it does. It's meant to.

I don't fear hurt as much as I fear never loving enough.

If you think, "If this doesn't work out, then I'll...," your leader will sense it. They'll be cautious to give you any real authority or let you get too close. If you keep finding a closed door in your face, could it be that you have an escape route planned?

If God led you to a ministry, then He intends for you to commit. He intends for you to follow and plan your future with them. The invitation to become a disciple wasn't taken lightly by Jesus. He meant to be with them years after the initial invitation.

I know that as a leader, when I invite someone, I plan my life thinking of that person being there for years to come. In fact, I build those pictures on purpose. It's amazing how easily the love flows when you do that. It's easy to love someone you can picture at your wedding, the birth of your future children, and at your seventieth birthday party!

So then, where do you see yourself in five years? Are you ready to burn your escape route and commit? If so, then the Lord will open the doors.

If you can check off all seven protocols, then you're the kind of champion any leader would be honored to have at their back.

Let's move on to ditching the hindrances to your success as a prophetic champion.

CHAPTER 10

THE CHAMPION KILLER

There's an evil that undermines the sharp edge of a champion's sword. It doesn't conquer in combat, but infiltrates in times of abundance and peace.

Of all the works of satan, this one poses the greatest danger to your gifts, call, and anointing.

As King David rose to fame and fortune, those who suffered lack with him in the cave of Adullam rose with him. Before long, Joab wasn't the commander over a couple of rag-tags. He was a general of repute. In 2 Samuel 3, we see him forget his humble beginnings!

2 Samuel 3:25–27 Surely you realize that Abner the son of Ner came to deceive you, to know your going out and your coming in, and to know all that you are doing." And when Joab had gone from David's presence, he sent messengers after Abner, who brought him back from the well of Sirah. But David did not know it. Now when Abner had returned to Hebron, Joab took him aside in the gate to speak with him privately, and there stabbed him in the stomach, so that he died for the blood of Asahel his brother.

The greatest warfare you confront as a champion isn't the enemies without. Rather, you'll battle the demons within.

The spirit of vainglory stands ready to be the voice of approval you desperately crave.

Prophetic training is arduous to best equip you for the greatest evil: your flesh. Failure doesn't breed vainglory, success does. Visit this chapter often. This demonic force is rooted in pride and holds the devastating power against unity. Be on your guard. This chapter will keep your back covered.

HOW THE SPIRIT OF VAINGLORY GAINS A GRIP ON YOU

1. YOU TAKE AUTHORITY THAT WASN'T DELEGATED TO YOU

Joab had a smart mouth. Now, I don't know how you were raised, but I wouldn't dare speak to a teacher with the tone Joab used on David! "Surely you realize that Abner the son of Ner came to deceive you, to know your going out and your coming in, and to know all that you are doing."

He took it upon himself to correct the King's decision! Joab crossed the line between providing counsel and setting himself up as an authority. "Why shouldn't David listen to me?" I'm sure he said to himself. In the moment, his opinion was justified.

When you overstep your boundary of authority, you're playing with the devil. Be careful, warrior, because the spirit of vainglory is nipping at your heels.

While surviving in the wilderness, I bet Joab couldn't imagine betraying David. However, as we watch this spirit overtake him, we see a man surrender his sword to the enemy and lose his life, clinging to the horns of the altar in dishonor.

Watch that line, champion, and don't give the enemy a foothold!

2. YOU PLAY THE GAME OF COMPARISON

Joab wasn't just upset because David didn't take his advice. Firstly, David met with Abner without his knowledge. Now, there was some bad blood between the two of them. At first glance, you imagine the grudge Joab held was because of his little brother's death.

Think about this angle for a bit, though. Abner was the general of Saul's (and now Ishbosheth's) army. If David made a deal with Abner, who was to remain general once David ruled Israel? Joab wasn't about to surrender his position. He forgot his purpose to build the kingdom. His position became an idol he would bow down to from this moment on.

Joab felt threatened. No one deserved the position more than him. So, he took matters into his hands. That spirit had more than a foothold in his life. He put action to a sinful temptation.

Look, it's one thing to feel your apostle missed it. It's another to take things out of their hands. However, that's exactly what Joab did!

And when Joab had gone from David's presence, he sent messengers after Abner, who brought him back from the well of Sirah. But David did not know it. [14]

He tried to save David from making a terrible mistake. The enemy fueled his self-righteousness.

This is the danger of the spirit of vainglory. It feels so righteous. Joab fought a holy battle! He would save David... even from himself.

Once again, a reminder. It wasn't within his authority to make that call. What's so dangerous about this spirit is how right it feels. You don't imagine that you're opposing your apostle. Quite the contrary. You imagine yourself as the only one who has the courage to save him from himself.

However, God didn't make Joab king. He anointed David as King. It's not about what decision is correct. It's about delegated authority.

3. NEVER SATISFIED WITH YOUR PORTION

Galatians 5:26 Let us not become conceited, provoking one another, envying one another.

Why couldn't Joab be satisfied with his portion? He already held one of the highest positions in the kingdom. However, he wanted it all. He wanted Abner's share as well.

The spirit of vainglory gained full control, leading to Abner's death. Joab crossed a line no amount of forgiveness could heal between him and David.

They still tried to make it work, though. David held onto Joab, although I can imagine it must have felt very awkward after this.

When you've allowed vainglory to drive you to the point of doing something detrimental to the ministry, there's no going back. The damage is done. Of course, Jesus forgives. However, you cannot unsay or undo what you put your hands to.

Look at what satan's trying to steal from you, champion! Never forget that Joab was one of the greatest warriors of all time. A man of honor. A man of power. As he succumbed to this spirit, he lost respect.

He lost the love of his king. He lost the honor of his peers. This spirit seeks to strip you of the things Jesus processed you for.

Stop and reflect before taking another step. Get back into the Lord's presence and put away your frustrations and perceived righteous indignation.

4. SEPARATION FROM OTHERS IN THE CORPS

Joab pushed past common sense and began to walk a dark road that day. More and more, he separated from the other champions, until he befriended Adonijah and attempted a coup to overthrow David.

One step at a time, he moved outside that tight circle. You might recognize this in others. The champion who used to stand in the middle of the crowd, takes up a seat on the outskirts.

You miss meetings. You lose vision. You begin asking, "Why am I here anyway? No one recognizes what I bring to the table. No one respects my grace or my gifting."

Before long you're throwing posts on social media that read, "If you're not celebrated, you don't belong there."

You forget that you weren't called as a champion to be celebrated.

Jesus is meant to be celebrated!

Philippians 2:3 Let nothing be done through selfish ambition or **conceit**, but in lowliness of mind let each esteem others better than himself.

That word "conceit" is also translated as vainglory.

Conceit believes what satan whispers:

"They don't appreciate your anointing."
"They forget the price you paid to grow this ministry."
"I deserve to be acknowledged for the part I played."

You just stepped right into the enemy's playground, and so the games begin.

Those you considered blood-brothers become distant acquaintances. Satan only comes to steal, kill, and destroy. His hold on your life is meant to steal the relationships God intended for you.

5. DEATH KNELL: A CURSE FOLLOWS

2 Samuel 3:28–29 Afterward, when David heard it, he said, "My kingdom and I are guiltless before the LORD forever of the blood of Abner the son of Ner. Let it rest on the head of Joab and on all his father's house; and let there never fail to be in the house of Joab one who has a discharge or is a leper, who leans on a staff or falls by the sword, or who lacks bread."

Perhaps you assume the spirit of vainglory was sent to destroy your leaders and peers. No, prophet, its desire is for you.

David came through just fine. Joab's failure didn't hurt the kingdom. God always pitched up at the eleventh hour to pull David through. The spirit of vainglory lies to you. It whispers in your ear, saying that you're right and everyone else is wrong.

It has no intention of attacking your leader. Its desire is for you; to keep you in its grip. It wants you wallowing in self-pity. He wants to see you lay your sword down and your superpower laid to waste.

The spirit of vainglory is indeed a champion killer.

God won't be mocked. So, you split the ministry with a couple of rebels who agree with your cause. What then?

David's line was established for generations as God promised. Unfortunately, Joab didn't get to see his name inscribed in that foundation.

He could have been there to see Solomon's temple built.

He could have fallen under the power as the priests stood to minister.

Instead, he traded his sword for death at the hand of Benaiah.

He bled out at the hand of a brother who, in better times, would've died for him.

The spirit of vainglory isn't your friend. It seeks to strip you of your best qualities. Be wary of it. Get back into your lane. Take up your place alongside your peers.

1. REPENT

Begin with repentance. Joab remained indignant – refusing repentance.

2. SHUT THAT SUCKER UP!

Next, tell the voice of that spirit to shut up! Once your mind clears, a very different world will take shape in front of you. Never make a rash decision based on offense. Bind every voice of offense. Cast down every imagination.

3. NOW, LISTEN.

Remember, you're a prophet. You can hear from God. Once you shut the devil up, you're ready to get direction.

4. MAKE IT RIGHT WITH YOUR APOSTLE

Don't keep it awkward between the two of you. If there's been bad blood, repent before God and ask forgiveness from man.

5. RESTORE YOUR ALIGNMENT

What will it take to help things heal? Do you need more time in the Word? Will investment of your time into the vision help?

Recognize that once the spirit of strife and vainglory tricks you, your peers and apostle will be wary of you. They might not trust your first attempts to make things right. Especially if that apostle had many others treat him this way. Remain humble. Keep communication lines open. If needed, start right back at the beginning to make things right.

Remember champion, it's not about your position. It's about establishing the Kingdom. We're aligned for Kingdom purpose, not selfish desire. You can do this!

CHAPTER 11

THE DAY YOU EARN YOUR CODE NAME

When we lived in our ministry center in Descanso, California, we had access to a hiking trail. Part of our routine included morning hikes. Wrangle a team of former athletes to a hike, and before you know it, the competition is set. Who would make it back first?

Fortunately, I don't need to be fleet-footed to lead troops into battle. Which is fortunate, seeing as Rebekah and I were the final stragglers to stumble into the office.

2 Samuel 2:18 Now the three sons of Zeruiah were there: Joab and Abishai and Asahel. And Asahel was as fleet of foot as a wild gazelle.

ASAHEL THE FLEET-FOOTED

Asahel was one of David's mighty men. And like a couple of strapping young men on my team, he knew how to run.

Unfortunately, his story didn't have a happy ending. He pursued the wrong warrior (Abner), and when it came down to it, paid for being in the wrong place at the wrong time with his life (2 Sam. 2:21-23).

Prophets crave the freedom of a unique identity. It's a spiritual law.

James 1:25 But he who looks into the perfect law of liberty and continues in it, and is not a forgetful hearer but a doer of the work, this one will be blessed in what he does.

James tells us that freedom is a law. God put it within us to crave freedom to run the race. Today, you'll learn what it takes to be truly unique.

Let's consider another five of David's champions. It's difficult not to imagine each one in a superhero series with origin stories, each more fantastical than the next.

Scripture only outlines their superpowers. I wonder, "what's your story, Eleazar? Who taught you to strap a sword like that?" Their metrics stood them apart within the champion corps.

It's only when you compare the swordsman to the lion killer, that you can truly appreciate the diversity they bring to the table.

ELEAZAR THE SWORDSMAN

2 Samuel 23:10 He arose and attacked the Philistines until his hand was weary, and his hand stuck to the sword. The Lord brought about a great victory that day; and the people returned after him only to plunder.

This was a man born with a sword in his hand. He didn't "warrior up" overnight. I imagine years of training made him into a champion.

Now, here's a curious thing. When Saul took the throne, iron was a new invention and only he and Jonathan possessed swords.

Where did Eleazar's sword come from? What was its name? I can imagine it had many stories to tell.

Eleazar stood apart - a man of tremendous discipline and skill. Yes, a brute. However, a brute with the focus to plough through every work of the enemy until the job was done.

SHAMMAH THE DEFENDER

2 Samuel 23:11 And after him was Shammah the son of Agee the Hararite. The Philistines had gathered together into a troop where there was a piece of ground full of lentils. So the people fled from the Philistines.

The Scripture doesn't tell us his weapon of choice. There's no doubt in my mind this man picked a fight with those Philistines. I bet they didn't see it coming.

Every corps needs that one guy who's willing to pick a fight and see it through. If ever someone shouted at dawn, "Hey anyone wanna start some trouble with me?" Shammah was your man!

BENAIAH THE LION KILLER

2 Samuel 23:20 Benaiah was the son of Jehoiada, the son of a valiant man from Kabzeel, who had done many deeds. He had killed two lion-like heroes of Moab. He also had gone down and killed a lion in the midst of a pit on a snowy day.

I'm from Africa. I've touched a lion. One doesn't nonchalantly approach the big cat and tickle its whiskers. Man-eaters roam the flatlands of Africa, and they demand fear and respect. How much more in an era when weapons weren't as available?

Then we have good old Benaiah. He wasn't easily intimidated by any roar of the enemy. After Shammah picked a fight and stirred up the lion men, it was Benaiah they called on for help.

He didn't even let the snow deter him. Did he even know the meaning of fear?!

ABISHAI THE SPEARMAN

2 Samuel 23:18 Now Abishai the brother of Joab, the son of Zeruiah, was chief of another three. He lifted his spear against three hundred men, killed them, and won a name among these three.

Every corps needs a sniper. Abishai was Asahel's brother, and I wonder if he ran like a gazelle. Do you recognize the Word is very particular about their skill sets?

If these men were invited to a birthday party, you might not recognize their diversity. A warrior is a warrior. They all need a shave, and their shirts are still stained with blood.

They diversified when they stood on the battlefield. It's only when you fight alongside others that you recognize your full potential to slay your God-given way.

JOSHEB-BASSHEBETH (JOSH) THE RUTHLESS

2 Samuel 23:8 These are the names of the mighty men whom David had: Josheb-Basshebeth the Tachmonite, chief among the captains. He was called Adino the Eznite, because he had killed eight hundred men at one time.

A final mention must be made of Josh. I can't help it. His name and deed bring to mind a terror who didn't stop until a blood-river flowed. You need to flip a certain switch in your head to drop this many men in a day.

Did he count as he went? Could he even count to 800? Who counts while slaying?

Who did the counting here? Then we remember – they fought as a corps. He dropped 'em while someone else counted 'em. Everyone had a place. They knew Josh would plough through while Shammah took out high ranking officials of skill.

WHAT'S YOUR CODE NAME?

Your freedom is found within the corps. It's only when you stand alongside others who share your passion that you discover your sword.

You can't be unique by yourself. You need at least one other person to compare yourself to.

It's time to come out of the wilderness. You keep testing your sword against members. It's time to stretch yourself.

If you want to find your code name, get onto the battlefield. Don't be like Asahel and go out on your own. Take the corps with you. Allow them to cover your back. Learn from them. Compare yourself to them.

Complete freedom comes the day you compare what you see in the mirror to what you see in the face of your peers.

You're different. You have something to bring to the table.

You, my friend, are a prophetic champion!

PART 3: RANK FORMATIONS

CHAPTER 12

THE CHAMPION WHO LAYS THEIR SWORD AT YOUR FEET

1 Samuel 18:4 And Jonathan took off the robe that was on him and gave it to David, with his armor, even to his sword and his bow and his belt.

When I cried out to God about conflicts in my team, He gave me a vision. I saw myself standing in a field. A mighty warrior walked up to me and laid their sword at my feet.

Jonathan did this with David as a covenant act. With this act he said, "My life is your life. Let's travel this road together."

The sword has always held tremendous significance to man.

Of all the weapons of warfare, it's the one most imbued with personality. In ancient texts, swords are given wills and human character traits.

If you consider that a sword was used in close combat, it makes sense. The sword saw a side of the warrior no one else did. Every sword has a story to tell.

When the Lord gave me the vision of the mighty warriors putting their sword at my feet, He gave me a message.

I was to look for a champion who would share their life with me.

Someone who offered me who they were and not what everyone else wanted them to be.

God wanted me to find champions who weren't afraid to lay their strengths and badges at my feet.

This revelation changed everything.

WHAT HAPPENS WHEN YOU CAN'T SAY NO

I had a character flaw, though. I wanted to give everyone a chance. A rejected prophet like me couldn't imagine saying no to someone who wanted to be on my team.

So, I didn't.

I took them all in. I drew in all the rebels who'd been hurt by the status quo church. I heard all the stories. Pastors who had affairs. Pastors who rejected their prophets for speaking God's message. Pastors who dominated their members.

Apostles exposed as cult leaders. Leaders who stole money and skipped the country...

Seemed to me every time a leader messed up, their mistake poured out on my front lawn. I understood. I loved. I ministered. And then, I got taken out.

I had so many Absaloms in my ministry, I couldn't keep track.

ABSALOM OR CHAMPION?

When God shared that I needed a champion who laid their sword at my feet, I realized I had it all wrong. I was laying my sword at everyone else's feet.

I loved training my team, but it was all I did. I'd minister to one hurt, only to trigger the next. I'd deliver them from one demon, only to find another seven ready to pounce.

I stopped writing. I stopped producing new materials. I halted my mandate and spent all day investing my sword into a handful of people who were sure to change the world.

The end result? Only the team got ministry! The body of Christ was left in the cold while I played house.

What happens when you don't do things God's way? Chaos! The team was in conflict. I wasn't getting any sleep. Our finances were in the toilet. Something needed to change.

MAKE THE DISTINCTION

I began making a distinction between members and champions. I didn't expect a member to lay their sword at my feet. I got it. They were members. They wouldn't share the same commitment to the work as me.

Their primary focus was to receive.

Members are takers of the sword. Champions are givers of the sword.

When I made this distinction, my team came to order overnight. What shocked me most wasn't the sudden halt of spiritual warfare. What hurt most was the effect this mistake had on the champions who remained.

They were as exhausted as me. They were also neglected. I spent all my time, even into the early hours, bandaging members, while my champions waged war uncovered.

It was time to clean house, and when I did, something miraculous happened. Order. Unity. A corps of gladiators at my back.

EMBRACE DIVERSITY

1 Chronicles 12:23-38 Now these were the numbers of the divisions that were equipped for war, and came to David at Hebron to turn over the kingdom of Saul to him, according to the word of the Lord: of the sons of Judah bearing shield and spear, six thousand eight hundred armed for war; [...]

All these men of war, who could keep ranks, came to Hebron with a loyal heart, to make David king over all Israel; and all the rest of Israel were of one mind to make David king.

When David's time came, each tribe brought their sword to his feet. Read the long list and recognize their diversity. Some brought spears and swords. Other tribes contributed chiefs of superior leadership skills.

As an apostle, you want this diversity.

A house full of evangelists will be on fire but never bring healing. A house of teachers will feed you bread but dry you out.

Don't assume everyone wants to be a chief. Many are adept at being foot soldiers. I lost some good people because I thrust them into leadership roles they weren't graced for.

We often think as leaders, if we just give someone a chance, the position will create in their reflection the warrior we see in the spirit.

Don't put a member into a champion's armor. Both of you will be crushed in the process.

When they fall apart, you will feel you failed as a leader. They will be bitter at you and hate their inadequacies.

So, to save everyone the heartache, I already gave you some clear-cut principles to differentiate between a member and a champion (see Chapter 3 - The Champion Model).

Now that we've cleared this level of accountability, I want to give you the first round of boot camp strategies for champions.

Problem is, if you try to take a member through boot camp, neither of you will make it. So, before you apply any sort of pressure on your potential champion, let's make sure they belong in the ranks in the first place.

CHAPTER 13

NEXT UP: CHAMPION BOOT CAMP

From the moment you take on your first champion, your relationship shifts from friend, pastor, spiritual parent... to coach.

Coaches aren't famous for their ability to score a goal. They're famous for their ability to train their star player to score a goal.

It's true, not every coach shares their team's talents. They might not be as fast or strong. He has this singular quality as a coach – he knows how to recognize potential and increase its capacity!

Hopefully your corps have skills that exceed yours. If so, you chose well. Some of them are faster. Some of them are stronger. Some of them are more intelligent.

Each position in the corps has a function.

Yours is to assemble the champions.
Then, it's for you to coach them.
Finally, it's for you to position them according to your mandate.

This isn't a competition to see who's better. King David was an incredible warrior. Yet, with his accolades, he stood like a withered reed next to Josh and Shammah.

He wasn't their king because he could bench press two hundred pounds. He was king because God anointed him to that position.

Never forget that you're appointed because of God's grace and not your merit.

When you enter the relationship from this perspective, then you're in a position to increase your team's potential.

REMEMBER WHERE YOUR CHAMPIONS HAVE BEEN

Keep in mind, some of your champions come from leaders who felt small in their shadow. What do small men do in the presence of greater men? Attack like a thief in the night.

They've survived more than one knife in the back. Approach with caution and a healthy dose of grace.

There isn't room for your insecurities to peek from under the covers. Your champion's sword should be celebrated. Challenged, yes, but celebrated!

Remember, it's because their sword was tested that they belong in the corps. Now it's up to you to coach them on how to practically apply their training to your mandate.

WORK THAT SWORD!

What's the first thing a coach makes a talented athlete do?

Push-ups. Sprints.

My son, Dalton Beckering, achieved a college football scholarship. His coach didn't care whether he was cold, hungry, or needed to use the bathroom. He was expected to be on the field at the crack of dawn for training.

He had to earn his position. He was put up against players bigger and better than him. So, he had to work harder and be faster. His coaches weren't fair. They weren't in play to make him feel good about himself. They were there to make him better for the game.

We accept that a worldly coach would and should push us to our limits. So, why hold back when the fate of the Kingdom lies in your hands?

The more your champion has to offer, the more coaching he needs.

The ones with the most potential are the most work and worth the most effort!

SUBMISSION. OBSERVANCE. SERVICE

Coaching your champions begins with three simple disciplines to which I've given the acronym: **SOS**

It stands for:

- ⇨ Submission
- ⇨ Observance
- ⇨ Service

Many leaders get so excited by having someone on their team, they march them right onto the field.

If you hand out tasks without any form of introduction into the corps, you invite chaos.

For every player to qualify, he brings his sword to the ranks.

A THREE TO NINE MONTHS TRAINING DISCIPLINE SHOULD BE DELIBERATE

If you position a champion because of skill set before you tried him with SOS, you're in for another wilderness wandering.

You'll eventually get there. Over time, your champion will rise to the challenge, but it will take years.

Submit them to a three to nine months integration system, rather than run the gauntlet with them until they learn the lessons by trial and error.

Be deliberate in training your team in SOS!

Any champion who's adept at any of these disciplines will always excel. Doors will always open. Promotions will chase after them. These are three spiritual laws our patriarchs took turns to bench-press.

It's what shaped them for mandate. Allowing your champion an escape from boot camp does them a disservice. Don't drop the ball on the coaching phase.

Trace the pattern of these disciplines through the Word with me.

EXAMPLES FROM THE WORD WHO APPLIED SOS

MOSES AND JETHRO

Exodus 18:7 So Moses went out to meet his father-in-law, bowed down, and kissed him. And they asked each other about their well-being, and they went into the tent.

Moses led over two million souls out of Egypt. He was kind of a big deal in his day. The head honcho. When his father-in-law arrived, he humbled himself before the man.

As Jethro shared counsel on the establishment of the judicial system, Moses obeyed.

It gives us insight to their relationship before Moses left for Egypt. This was a man content to stay in the wilderness and serve Jethro for the rest of his days.

God called on his humility at the burning bush. Moses was faithful to shepherd the sheep in the wilderness. This qualified him to lead the millions to the Promised Land.

DAVID AND SAUL

1 Samuel 16:21 So David came to Saul and stood before him. And he loved him greatly, and he became his armorbearer.

David defies logic in his handling of Saul - the dominating pastor who sent a hit squad after him. And yet still, he loves and serves. Had Saul embraced David, there's no doubt he would have gone right on back to the courts with his banner waving high.

David served God's people with the same humility he showed Saul. He put weight to his position by being a well-disciplined champion of submission, observance, and service.

PAUL AND GAMALIEL

Acts 22:3 "I am indeed a Jew, born in Tarsus of Cilicia, but brought up in this city at the feet of Gamaliel, taught according to the strictness of our fathers' law, and was zealous toward God as you all are today.

Teacher's pet. First thought that comes to mind when I think of Paul and Gamaliel. Apostle Paul could pen a killer letter, which, no doubt, stemmed from his obvious education.

First, a letter to assign Christians to jail. Then another to give them the keys to escape.

As a disciple to the Pharisee, Paul was expected to learn, obey, and pass the tests, just as Jesus expected of His disciples.

Whilst not voted the "most likely to make friends," Paul proves his qualification to us by always taking the lower seat.

He elevates Timothy and Silas to speak as his equals. He makes his own money to save the church another expense.

He submits his doctrine to the apostles in Jerusalem for vetting. His willingness to submit to their oversight says volumes of his character.

You aren't born with such character. You're trained into it. Today, you're the coach, required by God to train your team. Not to elevate yourself, but to launch your champion to success.

TIMOTHY AND PAUL

1 Thessalonians 3:2 and sent Timothy, our brother and minister of God, and our fellow laborer in the gospel of Christ, to establish you and encourage you concerning your faith,

Timothy didn't inherit his spiritual dad's ministry by tithing well. He became the man for the job through trial and testing.

He served Apostle Paul diligently. He obeyed when instructed to re-teach Paul's doctrine.

He served to bring Paul a coat when winter shook his old bones (2 Tim. 4:13).

The tenderness of Paul's expression each time he mentions Timothy speaks volumes of their relationship.

This is something a lot of leaders don't get. When a champion navigates integration and shares your passion for Christ, they join more than the corps.

They take up residence in your heart. They condition you as much as you condition them. Timothy surrendered his vision to embrace Paul's. A true spiritual son.

Next Up: Champion Boot Camp

You don't qualify as a son if you've never served as a champion.

JACOB AND LABAN

Genesis 31:41–42 Thus I have been in your house twenty years; I served you fourteen years for your two daughters, and six years for your flock, and you have changed my wages ten times. Unless the God of my father, the God of Abraham and the Fear of Isaac, had been with me, surely now you would have sent me away empty-handed. God has seen my affliction and the labor of my hands, and rebuked you last night."

Laban was a ruthless coach! He demanded metrics at any cost. When Jacob didn't play ball, Laban wanted his head.

Regardless, Jacob left the tents of Laban different from the man who entered.

Jacob left Esau with his brother's birthright in tow. He was a snotty little brother who couldn't even make his own deceiving stew.

Fast forward, two wives and a lifetime of punishment. He leaves Laban as the man of his home and future tribes tucked in his tent. He marched home as a man who surrendered to Laban's will time and again. He observed the rule. He served faithfully for over twenty years.

His reward never came from Laban. It came from Almighty God. We don't submit, observe, and serve because man rewards us. We do so for our own spiritual discipline. Our reward always comes from the Father.

Tell me, apostle, who was your Laban? Perhaps today you can let your offenses go. Had Laban not been the grueling coach he was, Jacob could never become the player who scored in the end.

Focus on the discipline. Whom did God require you to submit to? Whom did you obey? How many have you served? Each of these disciplines qualify you to coach the next generation of champions.

CHAPTER 14
SOS: SUBMISSION

Modern soldiers see but a fraction of their enemy. Spread out over hundreds of miles, they lean on their machines to do the work. Wars stretch on for years, delivering bombs and targeted assaults.

In antiquity, this wasn't the case. An enlisted soldier didn't fight many battles in his lifetime. When he was called to war, the enemy didn't hide. The recruit confronted miles of armored madmen growling for blood. That soldier only knew one thing in the moment: terror.

Survival depended on strategic formation. Formations and tactics had two purposes: give each champion the conviction that his formation would protect him, then convince the enemy that their formation couldn't protect them.

Don't believe everything you saw in Braveheart. Battle lines weren't a wild, free-for-all. Infantry fights could last for hours. Not many could maintain full strength that long. So, they sparred in short bursts. Facing one enemy at a time.

When the champion rested, he sparred behind a shield, flanked by his peers to the left, right, and rear. For as long as he held formation, the battle was a success. He caught his breath, headed beyond his shield and took ground.

Apostle, this is what submission looks like.

THE DISCIPLINE OF SUBMISSION IS A SURVIVAL SKILL FOR WAR

1 Peter 5:5–8 Likewise you younger people, submit yourselves to your elders. Yes, all of you be submissive to one another, and be clothed with humility, for "God resists the proud, but gives grace to the humble." Therefore humble yourselves under the mighty hand of God, that He may exalt you in due time, casting all your care upon Him, for He cares for you. Be sober, be vigilant; because your adversary the devil walks about like a roaring lion, seeking whom he may devour.

Strongs 5293. hupŏtassō,
to subordinate; reflex. to obey:
be under obedience (obedient),
put under, subdue unto, (be, make) subject (to, unto),
be (put) in subjection (to, under), submit self unto. [15]

War wasn't won by the strongest force. It was won by the force that kept their wits about them. In the time this Scripture was written, battle was fought in tight spaces. A champion saw only the enemy to kill and his peers, pressed in on every side. He trusted his general for positioning and his peers to alert him of danger.

Confidence in his peers determined his resolve. For the enemy to devour, he needed a scare tactic. Something to rattle the champion, to make him break rank and begin a fear cascade through the army.

We saw this play out as the Israelites trembled in their tents in 1 Samuel 17. Goliath belted out threats. A typical psychological warfare tactic!

How quickly did this switch when his head fell from his shoulders? Shock rippled through the Philistine army. Every general knew, once a soldier lost his nerve, the real killing began.

Infantry or cavalry in pursuit cut down any fleeing soldier.

The Philistines didn't fare well that day.

When 1 Peter 5 tells us to clothe ourselves with humility, it's saying: armor up! Submission to your elders and peers is that armor.

You can only see what's in front of you. No champion sees the full battlefield in array. They're dependent on one another.

The general can give the champion a position, but their continued submission to one another will decide whether they claim the victory.

A CAUTIONARY TALE- WATCH FOR WOLVES

I've had many through the years eagerly submit to my leadership. When I brought them into the ranks, they had a hard time submitting to their peers.

Instead, they competed. They vied for attention and control. They rebuffed every suggestion or teaching point. They weren't champions in the end. They weren't even members.

They were wolves sent amongst sheep and they devoured many.

THE POISON TIPPED ARROW: REBUFF

Rebuff: *A peremptory refusal of a request, offer, etc.: snub.* [16]

How've you been sleeping lately, apostle? Something that steals your rest is likely the continual rebuffs you get in your ministry and workplace.

They come most during the submission discipline. I'm about to help you sleep better at night.

"Could you send this letter out for me?"

"Sure, but it'll need to wait until I'm finished doing something else."

"God said we need to stand firmly in faith for this financial provision."

"Amen, apostle! I think that it would also be a good idea to consider taking out a loan as well. After all, the natural comes before the spiritual."

Fill in your dialogue. How many rebuffs did you get before you picked up this book today?

I love the dictionary definition. Every rebuff can also be named a "snub."

1. FIRST COMES THE REBUFF

It takes a bit to get, "Wait a minute! Did you just snub me?!"

Sneaky! It's a roll of the eyes; an arrogant smirk that whispers, "I know better."

It's a hand in your face.

The reason why you don't spot it anymore is because you're desensitized to it. When you had only one champion to coach, you could handle it. Rebuff from three or more, positions you as a punching bag in center ring. You're gonna bleed.

NEXT, YOU PICK UP THEIR LEAVEN

1 Corinthians 5:8 Therefore let us keep the feast, not with old leaven, nor with the leaven of malice and wickedness, but with the unleavened bread of sincerity and truth.

Luke 12:1–2 …"Beware of the leaven of the Pharisees, which is hypocrisy. For there is nothing covered that will not be revealed, nor hidden that will not be known.

Rebuffs are spiritual war cries against you. Their arrows are tipped with discontent, malice, and offense. They're the weapon of a champion who hasn't disciplined himself in submission.
    If you leave it unchecked, it will poison you. Their unspoken disagreement whispers questions in your head.
    "I wonder why they said that?"
    "Am I reading too much into this?"
    "If I address it, what do I say? It wasn't that obvious."
    Let's get real. We all know a rebuff when it stabs us in our vulnerability. An invisible hand slapped you. You feel poked at, made fun of.
    You just got poisoned and you took it! You won't sleep well.

NOW, YOU QUESTION YOURSELF

Psalms 140:3 They sharpen their tongues like a serpent; the poison of asps is under their lips.

The poison works its evil magic. You question your decisions. Self-doubt. Fear.
    Stop right there. You just got rebuffed and it's time to shake free!

STOP THE REBUFF!

Don't believe the lies. Go back to what God told you. Reboot.
It's already too late to address the rebuff if it happened yesterday. So, let it lie.
I promise, if that champion rebuffed you before, it'll happen again. Likely soon. This time prepare yourself.

CALL OUT THE REBUFF

Rebuffs lose their power when you call it out in the moment. Stop the arrow before it penetrates. Don't go home to ponder on it. Catch it as it flies.
The sooner you call it out, the sooner it stops. Most champions don't realize they're doing it. If they continue to do it after being highlighted many times, you should weigh in on their champion versus member status.

FOLLOW THROUGH WITH MINISTRY

Look deeper than the rebuff. Calling it out isn't meant to shut the champion up. It's meant to highlight a hidden problem.
You don't know whether it stems from insecurity or bitterness. So, go deeper. Call it out and then ask questions.
Remember, when you allow a champion in your ranks who refuses to arm themselves with humility, they're the one to buckle first. Their loss of confidence sends a signal throughout the ranks, tempting others to tremble.
The Strongs definition of submission clearly states: "to subject yourself to."[17]
In rookie terms, it means to:

1. Be deliberate in putting your peers above yourself.
2. Go with someone else's idea.

3. Listen to someone else's input for the purpose of finding value.
4. Trust that your team has your back.
5. Rejoice when your peer is promoted. Weep with them when they fall.
6. Put your peers ahead of yourself for promotion.
7. Consider that you see just your part of the battlefield. You need your peer's perspective also.

LET'S MAKE IT PRACTICAL

Remember, submission is a discipline that requires boundaries and expectations. I'll share our practice with you, and you're welcome to glean what fits your ministry.

When a new champion steps into our lives, they do so having already qualified. Most likely, they graduated one of our schools.

Once they're invited to the team, they're made to shadow one of our existing champions. Craig and I seek God to find a mandate match. They go through three months of integration.

Their champion mentor teaches them our protocols, systems, and expectations. They also get the opportunity to work in all our ministry departments. We're keen to explore the strength of the sword they add to the ranks.

Now, most find it easy to submit to the apostles. Even if we need to voice a disapproval, they oblige. However, when the same instruction comes from a peer, their submission is sorely tested. In that moment, their battle readiness is measured.

Is this the kind of person we can leave on the battlefield with the team when we travel? Is this champion someone we can trust to cover their peers if we send them out?

THE RESULT

Once they arm themselves with humility, their spiritual armor gets an upgrade. We know it in an instant. Their shield locks in with their peers and our formation grows.

The result is tangible! The champion becomes confident in who they are within the ranks. They step out more. Their anointing increases. They know what their sword is, where to use it and that it's safe to use it.

They're confident because for the first time in their lives – they don't fight their battle alone.

Unfortunately, not all recruits make it. They want to use their sword without respect for the swords of others. They don't understand why we won't position them as a division leader and use their unique skill set.

We know the truth. The enemy that roars is easy to target. The enemy that rattles the troops threatens us all.

Don't just teach submission. Measure it. Test it. When you bring a new champion on board, make your expectations clear. Set the boundaries and allow them the opportunity to succeed and also fail.

If you allow them the time to learn submission in a safe environment:

1. If they fail, your ministry isn't damaged.
2. They appreciate the value of their hard work. This isn't an easy discipline to master, so once they do it, they should feel good about themselves.
3. Finally, laying it out gives your champion the excitement of the goal that's ahead. Learn the discipline, receive promotion.

It shouldn't take longer than three months for you to determine if they have what it takes. Be bold! Next up... Observance!

CHAPTER 15

SOS: OBSERVANCE

We couldn't find a publisher for my first book. So, we took the apostolic route. We self-published. Craig established our first in-house printing department in 2001.

Every book passed through our hands - from cover design, format, bind, and finally to box. My daughters grew up with the smell of lamination and hot paper reams.

It isn't a reach to imagine our second eldest, Jessica, as one of our first bookshop managers. I passed on the art of graphics design to her keen sense of style. She could print, bind, and ship a book in record time. She ran our book production division like a boss.

By her eighteenth birthday, she was a graduate of our pastor teacher school and the manager of book production and shipment.

As God added team members to our growing ministry, everyone took a turn to work in the bookshop. A sure-fire test of faith, hope, and love was to have a new team member placate a frustrated customer whose book was used as a soccer ball by UPS.

The real workout happened somewhere between the cover printer and book cutter.

Ever want to invite someone's opinion? Have them observe the instructions of a teenager.

THE DISCIPLINE OF OBSERVANCE

Hebrews 13:17 Obey those who rule over you, and be submissive, for they watch out for your souls, as those who must give account. Let them do so with joy and not with grief, for that would be unprofitable for you.

Titus 2:15 Speak these things, exhort, and rebuke with all authority. Let no one despise you.

Of all Jessica's challenges, the greatest was the lack of simple protocol observance for menial tasks. Every protocol was questioned by the new recruit. From stock taking to packaging standards.

Ask any of them to rate themselves on a scale of 1-10 on obedience and they would all give you an 11!

No one considered their uninvited opinions and questioning of her instructions as disobedience. Neither do we. We treat God that way all the time.

We skirt around the issue. Delay on taking a step. We wait around for "more revelation." All the while, walking in disobedience to His instruction.

It's easy to spot. Just look for excuses on why tasks couldn't be done. If you have more excuses than metrics, then what you are is disobedient.

Well, our new recruits did just that. They made excuses as to why books were shipped late. They gave opinions on how boxes should be taped. In fact, the incoming opinions took so long... shipping was delayed.

SOS: Observance

A simple instruction from Jessica became a call to war. They were champions. They had so much more to offer. Unfortunately, what they didn't have, was the discipline of observance.

Sales increased and she created a systematic shipment system. A helpful new recruit added an opinion and their ideas on a better way to organize shipment. Their plan cost us hundreds of dollars. A number of packages were switched and shipped thousands of miles ... to the wrong country!

Protocol observance isn't a power play. It's a survival essential for your corps. If you don't create an environment to teach it, you'll lose a lot more than a few hundred dollars. You put lives on the line.

UNINVITED OPINIONS ARE DISOBEDIENCE

Titus 3:1-2 Remind them to be subject to rulers and authorities, to obey, to be ready for every good work, to speak evil of no one, to be peaceable, gentle, showing all humility to all men.

"How many times do I need to remind you...?" That's pretty much what Paul told Titus to say.

"Remind them to have some humility!"

"Zip your lip on uninvited opinions and live at peace with others!"

As a ministry leader, you've been assailed with your fair share of opinions. Usually from those who've never begun a ministry.

You've had some attempt to school you on doctrine, whose local church is a facebook page.

They have no metric for their opinion, so it holds no power. These are people who've never learned the discipline of observance. Because they never observed the laws of others, they build lives around their own.

WHAT IS PROTOCOL OBSERVANCE?

To follow the instruction set before you, by a person of authority - to the letter of the law.

Back in the day, we shipped our manuals out with lecture audio CDs.

They fit into a CD sleeve at the back of the manual.

One helpful recruit followed all instructions on CD and manual creation. Before shipment, they glued the CD to the front of the manual instead of the back - creasing the cover.

Did they observe the protocols?

CD was made. Manual was made. Package was shipped. Pity about the trashed front cover.

When we leave a ring of the tabernacle curtain out of our pattern, the Father says, "Reboot!" You know the pressure on your shoulders to get things right.

So, give your champions a head start. Teach them observance while they're still in boot camp. That way, when they take to the battlefield, they obey God organically.

A GOOD PLACE TO TEACH OBSERVANCE

Find or create an environment that includes detail-oriented work. Have someone train them to get the task done, in order and according to protocols.

Someone who can follow orders in the bookshop is someone who will follow orders on the battlefield.

When you have someone manifesting a demon in front of you, the last thing you need is for them to break protocol.

ACCEPT INPUT BASED ON METRICS... ONLY AFTER BOOT CAMP

Your champions come packed to the hilt with sword power. They likely have incredible advice to give for all your ministry divisions. It's not the point. Can they observe the protocols you've already set before they qualify to write new ones with you?

Titus and Timothy are instructed by Apostle Paul to follow strict church protocols.

As such, they qualified to create new ones alongside him as the apostle to the Gentiles.

THE CHAMPION THAT'S EAGER TO CONTRIBUTE

You can always spot the new guy! He looks a bit like this:

"After he had drawn up his men-at-arms, one of them went out far in advance of the rest, and then was stricken with fear when an enemy advanced to meet him and went back again to his post. 'Shame on you, young man,' said Phocion, 'for having abandoned two posts, the one which was given you by the general, and the one which you gave yourself ' – Life of Phocion: 25" (Swanton, 2020, Introduction) [18]

Be patient. Your champion will find his place if you've arranged your boot camp system well.

A true champion is keen to help. They break past battle lines to deliver you revelations. They're so keen to impress, that before you finish a sentence, they'll offer their opinion.

If they're prophetic, they'll deliver that opinion with, "thus saith the Lord."

When you expect it, you'll lose less hair. It's only a sign of passion. Utilize their passion. Instruct them to observe protocols to the letter.

Repeat yourself.
Repeat yourself.
Repeat yourself... often.

Because that is what the observance discipline requires.

If you said it once, I can assure you, it won't be done to protocol.

It should be re-iterated, daily.

Observance to protocol allows you to fit all the pieces together. Each team in place. Each champion at their post.

Don't assign your champion to their permanent post until they've qualified in the discipline of submission and observance.

IS A NEW SWORD BEING FORGED THROUGH THIS FIRE?

Once your champion observes protocols, they're ready to contribute. Weigh their sword once again. Where do they show metrics?

I recommend giving them the opportunity to navigate all your ministry divisions. They'll find treasure in uncharted places. When Austin joined us, he was a goat farmer, studying to be a vet. He tried to convince me that his skill set lay mostly in manual labor (preferably outdoors).

SOS: Observance

Today he is the Gathering Place pastor (our hub in Rosarito, Mexico). Until I thrust him to the podium to preach, he never knew he had it in him!

Remember, apostle, the responsibility weighs on you to celebrate the champion's sword. The sword they bring to you might be one of yesterday. As they join your ranks, make it your mission to assess if God has a sword He's forging for their tomorrow, as part of this new team.

HOW TO DETERMINE WHEN THEY'VE MASTERED OBSERVANCE

1. They lose the appetite for giving everyone their opinion.
2. They follow instructions to the letter.
3. They complete their tasks with joy! Begrudging protocol observance is still disobedience. They must make the protocols their own.
4. They re-teach protocols to others exactly like they were taught. (No embellishment!)

CHAPTER 16

SOS: SERVICE

Matthew 8:8-9 The centurion answered and said, "Lord, I am not worthy that You should come under my roof. But only speak a word, and my servant will be healed. For I also am a man under authority, having soldiers under me. And I say to this one, 'Go,' and he goes; and to another, 'Come,' and he comes; and to my servant, 'Do this,' and he does it."

The chief strength of the Roman army was the legionary infantry. Qualification for rank was military experience and reputation for personal bravery.

In fact, this is what it took to become a centurion:

"The centurion in the infantry is chosen for his size, strength and dexterity in throwing his missile weapons and for his skill in the use of his sword and shield; in short for his expertness in all the exercises. He is to be vigilant, temperate, active and readier to execute the orders he receives than to talk; Strict in exercising and keeping up proper discipline among his soldiers, in obliging them to appear clean and well-dressed and to have their arms constantly rubbed and bright." (Vegetius. De Re Militari, II, 14) [19]

The centurion who approached Jesus knew his way around the battlefield. When Jesus offered to heal his servant, he said something peculiar.

RISE OF THE PROPHETIC CHAMPIONS

"For I also am a man under authority, having soldiers under me. And I say to this one, 'Go,' and he goes;" [20]

This is a man who served. In turn, he expected the men under him to serve. He understood the concept of being under authority. He qualified for his promotion. He qualified to send others into battle.

When you fail to qualify your champions, you send them into a battle they'll lose. Of all three disciplines, serving under authority qualifies a champion most.

It's the dividing line between mandate, life, and death. Many mistake servanthood as dishwashing. This is *Rise of the Prophetic Champions*. You already cleaned toilets and washed dishes while serving a pastor.

More is required. Did you see your battles through? A centurion was chosen from the ranks for his continued success and pursuit of the vision. He put his life aside time and again.

WHAT A SERVING CHAMPION LOOKS LIKE

No one whips us into shape quite like Apostle Paul! Romans 12 should be in every apostle's playbook.

INTENTIONS AREN'T ENOUGH

Romans 12:1 I beseech you therefore, brethren, by the mercies of God, that you present your bodies a living sacrifice, holy, acceptable to God, which is your reasonable service.

Apostles… where are the metrics? Good intentions don't save lives. Real actions with real effort do! There's a huge difference between offering to do a job and then actually doing it.

Expect your champions to put action to their intentions. God requires us to give up our bodies as living sacrifices. It isn't enough to "think holy thoughts." He demands action to our intention. If a champion offered to help in any way, did they follow through? If not, you got some coaching to do.

TEMPERATE

Romans 12:3 For I say, through the grace given to me, to everyone who is among you, not to think of himself more highly than he ought to think, but to think soberly, as God has dealt to each one a measure of faith.

There's no place for pride in the ranks. Pride turns champions against one another. It soon becomes a free-for-all, and everyone loses.

Don't feel bad if you missed this. The Father gave us a heart to love and heal. When a champion acts out, you want to help him feel loved and part of the team.

You can make the mistake of trying to placate him so much that you miss an obvious point. The champion fails because they aren't in their grace. Instead, they compare themselves to others and always feel like they fall short. Here are some phrases to watch out for:

"I just never feel like I'm good enough."

"Everyone else is so much better than me."

"I never seem to get anything right, no matter how hard I try."

"The others put me down."

These are warning phrases. Your champion needs to master the discipline of service. First to his peers, then to the vision.

RISE OF THE PROPHETIC CHAMPIONS

EXPERT IN ALL EXERCISES

2 Timothy 2:3–5 You therefore must endure hardship as a good soldier of Jesus Christ. No one engaged in warfare entangles himself with the affairs of this life, that he may please him who enlisted him as a soldier. And also if anyone competes in athletics, he is not crowned unless he competes according to the rules.

List the pillars of your ministry. A centurion got his place by being an expert in all forms of battle. We all have a favorite battle plan. We also know that battle plans aren't a "one size fits all."

The way you cast that demon out today will change when you're challenged with someone else. You want a champion who challenges himself to excellence. If he's still sharing the same testimony today as he did five years ago, he needs an upgrade.

This is the hobby horse danger. Hobby horses have a very short lifespan. Cultures shift, and if you get stuck on your hobby horse, you don't realize when everyone goes motorized and you get left behind.

Champions are keen to learn new skills and evolve with the vision.

LOYALTY

2 Timothy 2:2 And the things that you have heard from me among many witnesses, commit these to faithful men who will be able to teach others also.

Apostle:

- ⇨ Offering your platform won't breed loyalty.
- ⇨ Open ministry doors won't breed loyalty.
- ⇨ A vote of confidence won't breed loyalty.
- ⇨ Loving on a champion won't breed loyalty.
- ⇨ Weeks of deliverance won't breed loyalty.
- ⇨ Ridiculous amounts of financial investment won't breed loyalty.

Now, don't misunderstand me. I'm not saying you should avoid these things. Rather, I'm saying that either loyalty is a strand of a champion's DNA or it isn't.

Apostle Paul instructed Timothy to seek out faithful men for their message. You can teach a champion the mechanics of faithfulness. However, loyalty is a decision of their heart. It can be nurtured once they have it.

It's not your mandate to impart loyalty. As an apostle, it's your responsibility to model it to those who've gone before you.

You cannot coach disloyalty out of a champion. Rather, you can work with the loyalty he has to offer.

HOW TO CREATE AN ENVIRONMENT TO COACH SERVICE

So, how does your team measure up? There's a simple test you can perform to gauge your champion's "servant meter."

HOW TO GAUGE THE CHAMPION'S "SERVANT METER"

You know your ministry best. Position your champion in each of these case scenarios. Grant them a score from 1-10.

⇨ 1 being that they didn't try the task at all.
⇨ 10 being that they completed the task with a fantastic attitude, in a timely manner.

1. Ask your champion to do something that's slightly beyond their ability.

We have a tendency to avoid tasks that highlight insecurity. A disciplined champion will attempt the task even if they expect failure.

This champion will think on their feet in battle. They set themselves up to be inner circle leadership.

2. Ask your champion to serve in a capacity that doesn't offer a reward.

Acts 9:15–16 But the Lord said to him, "Go, for he is a chosen vessel of Mine to bear My name before Gentiles, kings, and the children of Israel. For I will show him how many things he must suffer for My name's sake."

Why are we doing this again? When the Father invited Apostle Paul to ministry, it wasn't a pretty invitation. "Serve me Paul, and you will suffer."

One who serves well does so from the nucleus of their spiritual DNA. One who's in it for the acclaim will high-tail it the minute you don't give them a pat on the back.

3. Ask your champion to serve when it's very inconvenient.

A servant who works hard in the field returns home to serve again. Jesus was often weary when assailed by the masses. Each time He served (Mark 6:33-34).

One who can't serve without recognition will be the first to run for cover at the slight sign of danger.

FINAL WORDS ON THE CHAMPIONS OF SOS

Every champion has a favorite discipline. Although they should master all three, don't be surprised to see them lean more towards one.

A champion who's followed each season of boot camp through is one you can position in the ranks of the corps.

CHAPTER 17

ARRANGE YOUR CHAMPIONS IN RANK AND FILE

Everyone who's ever worked with a prophet knows this one thing: they have a low boredom tolerance.

No one wants to sign up for battle without a call to war. David's champions wanted to see action. If he left them bored for very long, they got antsy. Same with the corps.

There's no such thing as an inactive champion because an inactive champion is a rusty one. A rusty champion is a spiritually dying one. Let's stir them to action!

1. ARRANGE IN RANK

You're not a pew warmer. You're a cave dweller and battlefield general. Position is everything for a champion with a sword to offer.

Ask yourself, what can each champion do that you can't?

If they match you skill for skill, you aren't choosing well.

The last thing you need is a spare part in case one breaks down. Rather have five super soldiers, than one hundred foot soldiers who don't know who they are. Seek out the skill in your champions you lack.

APPLICABLE MILITARY FORMATION

Roman soldiers marched onto the field arranged in file and line.

A file was a straight line of eight to sixteen men. The front man broke ground. The second man carried a shield. Each man in file carried a rank and boasted a skill set. The back-man had the toughest job. He made sure everyone stayed in rank.

Figure 2: A file (Design by Jessica Toach, 2023)

That's a file.

Now imagine 1,000 files standing side by side, rank by rank. That's 1,000 front men breaking ground. That's 1,000 shield carriers holding ground. That's 1,000 back men keeping the line!

Arrange Your Champions in Rank and File

Figure 3: Several files standing side by side (Design by Jessica Toach, 2023)

Each soldier in file partnered with their counterpart to the left and right. This strategy kept Rome on top of the pecking order for just on 500 years. [21]

We could learn a thing or two about rank and file. If you send champions to run rampant, you undermine their skill set.

Recognize their rank. Position them accordingly.

In 2000, we didn't have a clue what a marketplace prophet was. I look back and cringe. I kept placing marketplace prophets in all the wrong places. I expected them to preach, when they were called to cut a deal. Both of us felt let down. When you don't recognize your champion's rank and position them accordingly, you both lose out.

Don't make a prophet preach if his sword is deliverance. Don't ask the preaching prophet to spend hours in counseling sessions. It's not your job to "stretch them," it's your job to respect and position their sword accordingly.

2. THE FATAL FLAW: WHERE NOT TO POSITION

When you know what a champion doesn't have, you see better what they do!

The front-man requires boldness. The back-man requires vigilance. Be unafraid to test a champion in their weakest place. I give the opportunity for everyone to preach, prophesy, pray and administrate in my ministry. I'm learning. When I know your weak link, I know your rank in the file.

It's good for all of us to know our fatal flaws... that one thing that always trips us up. Blinding ourselves to our fatal flaw sets us up for perpetual failure.

Face your reality. Flaws are okay! That's why we're in rank and file! We have a buddy at our back.

My heart's strength is bound up in its ability to pump blood through my veins. It's limited when it comes to inhaling oxygen because that's the role my lungs play. Yet together, every organ in the body is oxygenated.

Is your corps full of life?

Position each according to superpower and fatal flaw and you've got an army.

2 Corinthians 12:9 And He said to me, My grace is sufficient for you, for My strength is made perfect in weakness. Therefore most gladly I will rather boast in my infirmities, that the power of Christ may rest upon me.

Come to terms with your limitations. Come to terms with the limitation of each champion.

Arrange Your Champions in Rank and File

WHEN FATAL FLAWS BECOME... FATAL

Revisit our imagery of the Roman army formation. Picture yourself as the fifth in file.

You have a soldier to your left, right, front, and back. View is limited. You trust your ears to carry the story of what's going on ahead.

Lack of talent didn't lose wars. It was the inability to keep rank. If the enemy could cause man number five to panic, he could influence everyone along the line. Fear breeds chaos. Instead of forging ahead as a unit, men begin to turn on one another and before long, friendly fire takes the life of half the regiment!

If you have a champion who keeps sparking a stampede, you have a problem.

So, when do you cover a flaw and when do you address it? Answer the questions below.

APPLICATION:

List the most obvious fatal flaw of each champion.

    a. Does this flaw impact the ministry negatively?
    b. Does this flaw trip up others in rank?
    c. Does this flaw prevent personal spiritual growth (Demonic bondages and sinful habits apply)?
    d. Does this flaw cut against your vision for the ministry?

If the answer is *no* to all of these, then let sleeping flaws lie. Just because you see a fault, doesn't mean you need to address it. Jesus sees all our flaws and yet waits years at a time to address them! Have the same grace.

On the other hand, if the answer is *yes* to any of these questions, your champion has some growing to do. You'll need to point it out to them and then offer a solution on how to overcome.

Make use of the following application to help a champion balance their flaw with a strength.

Arrange Your Champions in Rank and File

APPLICATION:

Take the list you made of your champion's flaws.

Now list the antonym of that flaw:

For example:

- ⇨ Talk too much. Antonym: to listen.
- ⇨ Act without thinking. Antonym: to set structure.
- ⇨ Harsh when they speak to people. Antonym: use tact.
- ⇨ Gives opinion. Antonym: Take time to get revelation from the Lord.

Once you have the antonym of their flaw, their training begins.

You cannot train a fatal flaw out of someone. Rather, train a new skill into them. This is apostolic leadership!

CHAPTER 18

COACH. POSITION. IMPART

Romans 1:11–12 For I long to see you, that I may impart to you some spiritual gift, so that you may be established - that is, that I may be encouraged together with you by the mutual faith both of you and me.

1 Thessalonians 2:8 So, affectionately longing for you, we were well pleased to impart to you not only the gospel of God, but also our own lives, because you had become dear to us.

The use of this word "impart" means to hand over something you own. In Luke 3:11, it's used in context of owning two tunics. Jesus instructs us to give a tunic to someone who doesn't have one.

So, when Apostle Paul says, "I want to impart the gospel and our lives to you," he means, "I want to give a piece of myself away to you."

There's nothing more apostolic than impartation. What champions don't comprehend is how much it costs us.

WHAT IMPARTATION COSTS THE APOSTLE

I was 100% prophet. When the Lord led me to teach, I dug in my heels. I didn't want any of that boring stuff. He pursued me. When I relented, He made it harder. He made me beg for that anointing.

I spent three solid years begging for the anointing to teach. I remember leaving my bed late at night and crying before the Father. I begged, "Father, without vision, the people perish. I can't impart without the anointing to teach!" Every time I preached the anointing fell short. So, I prayed. When my faith matched His promise, I stood to teach on the apostolic, and in the middle of my message, I stepped into the glory cloud. I felt as if I was standing and watching myself teach. God gave me what I travailed for. Things moved very quickly after that. Within a year, I wrote the entire *Prophetic Field Guide series*. I taught 22 courses in our Fivefold Ministry Campus. I could hardly keep up with the revelation download.

By the end of 2022, I had published 41 books and training manuals. I had produced over 400 teachings. The Next Gen Prophets Tribe was born, and God urged me higher. I felt that familiar call to change gears.

Producing training content had to shift towards coaching emerging NextGen apostles. I didn't realize just how much I clung to my teaching anointing until something happened at a prophetic conference in Denmark.

After a grueling preaching tour, the Lord told me, "You won't teach this all on your own. Tell Jessica to step up." I handed her the platform for two of the sessions. I then proceeded to make my way to Golgotha.

She stood up in the grace I carried. What took me years to master, she did effortlessly - with a double portion. I wasn't the only one who noticed. By the end of the conference, everyone referred to her messages over mine. I knew what God just did.

He lifted the mantle off me and placed it on her. On one hand, I couldn't be prouder. On the other, I knew I had imparted/given it away. God needs me to invest into new fields now.

The anointing to teach will always be a tool at my disposal, but the mantel has passed on. Now, to new territories: a new journey and impartation from the Father!

LEVELS OF IMPARTATION

As an apostle, God will have you navigate seasons to collect mantles. You'll fight for them. They'll become your best friends. And then… God will have you pass the mantle on.

It's because David handed the throne to Solomon that the Temple stood. The Jordan parted for Joshua because Moses handed over his mantle.

Before you jump on the impartation bandwagon, recognize the different levels.

LEVEL 1: IMPARTATION OF GIFTS

2 Timothy 1:6 Therefore I remind you to stir up the gift of God which is in you through the laying on of my hands.

Perform this level of impartation often. Every time God takes me up a level, its corps meeting time. I then lay hands and impart the portion of oil that God gave me.

As God takes me higher, they go higher with me. We evolve together. Paul held nothing back. Silas began as a preaching prophet and leveled up to a champion who wrote epistles with him.

Exodus 24:9–10 Then Moses went up, also Aaron, Nadab, and Abihu, and seventy of the elders of Israel, and they saw the God of Israel. And there was under His feet as it were a paved work of sapphire stone, and it was like the very heavens in its clarity.

Moses didn't keep the glory to himself. Once his place with the Father was secure, he took Joshua and the elders into the glory.

What did you receive? It's corps meeting time in the war room! Instruct, impart, and train them in the new anointing God gave you.

When God imparts a new toolset for deliverance, I hand it out as quick as I master it. The more you impart, the closer your unit becomes. Impartation nurtures team unity and enables champions to power up.

LEVEL 2: IMPARTATION OF AUTHORITY

Exodus 18:25–26 And Moses chose able men out of all Israel, and made them heads over the people: rulers of thousands, rulers of hundreds, rulers of fifties, and rulers of tens. So they judged the people at all times; the hard cases they brought to Moses, but they judged every small case themselves.

Authority is delegated. Impartation of authority is essential to ministry survival. Weigh the metrics of your champions and impart authority often.

Position them. Give them a vote of confidence. Do as Moses – announce their place publicly. Moses took the authority God gave him and imparted it to the elders to rule.

This requires laying on of hands and public announcement. To impart authority means to lay hands and to commission your champions to the work of God!

This happens at set times when the need arises. Moses imparted authority for a good reason. The nation of Israel was huge. He couldn't handle teaching the law by himself. In the same way, when you impart authority to your champions, your ministry grows.

You can't grow with a small ministry mindset. Impart authority to those who qualify according to your ministry growth.

LEVEL 3: IMPARTATION OF YOUR MANTLE

1 Kings 2:2–4 "I go the way of all the earth; be strong, therefore, and prove yourself a man. And keep the charge of the LORD your God: to walk in His ways, to keep His statutes, His commandments, His judgments, and His testimonies, as it is written in the Law of Moses, that you may prosper in all that you do and wherever you turn; that the LORD may fulfill His word which He spoke concerning me, saying, 'If your sons take heed to their way, to walk before Me in truth with all their heart and with all their soul,' He said, 'you shall not lack a man on the throne of Israel.'

Well done, good and faithful servant. When the end of a race comes into view, the beginning of another begins to stir.

An apostle's greatest failure is to miss the transition. We can become so faithful to our mandates that we forget we serve the Father.

When God brings a mandate to a close, it's time to impart the mantle to the next generation. Like Solomon, your champion will mess with your ideas of perfection.

WHEN THE NEXT GEN TAKE OVER...

When Jessica began creating content for our Fivefold Ministry Campus, she changed protocol and leadership structure completely. She "next genned" the graphics and swung the focus of our training towards emerging pastors and teachers. Joshua carried Moses' mantle, but he wasn't Moses.

He was a man of war while Moses was a man of humility. Solomon was a man of peace, where David was a man of war. Same mandate. Different season.

When you impart your mantle to the champion God points out to you, brace yourself. David designed a practical temple. Solomon blinged it out with filigree and hammered gold.

Deuteronomy 34:9 Now Joshua the son of Nun was full of the spirit of wisdom, for Moses had laid his hands on him; so the children of Israel heeded him, and did as the LORD had commanded Moses.

Another sign is this: People will follow the champion you mantled. If they don't, you didn't choose right. It didn't take long for others to seek Jessica out ahead of me for counseling principles. This was all the confirmation I needed.

Mantle imparted. New road up ahead.

COACH. POSITION. IMPART… REPEAT!

God created us to multiply. Of all the aspects, impartation is my favorite. Craig laid hands on Chaifa and imparted the anointing to minister to the broken-hearted. I imparted to Nate the anointing to lead. Austin received an impartation to preach and Mike, to cast out demons.

Every aspect of my journey has purpose, as does yours. No gift is wasted. Every anointing you paid a price for has merit.

The greatest impact we can have as apostles isn't in the display of our gifts. Rather, it's in the established work of the champions who double up on the anointing we carry.

Together, prophets and apostles are called to a battlefield. The lines are drawn. The battleplans imparted. Prophets are trained and at the ready.

So, let's prepare. Let's make way for the *Rise of Prophetic Champions*!

ABOUT THE AUTHOR

Writer, apostle, and spiritual mother to the prophets, Colette Toach is the author of 43 books about fivefold ministry training. Her top-selling book, *The Apostolic Handbook* is used at Wagner University as part of the Apostolic Leadership Course. Her online prophetic school has trained thousands of prophets since 1999. She and her husband Craig are recruited to ministries around the world to train fivefold ministry teams. She works every day to "write gooder" as her late spiritual father, Dr. Steve Greene used to say.

About the Author

LET'S BUILD A RELATIONSHIP

 Find out more about me:
www.toach-ministries.com

 Connect with me on Facebook:
www.facebook.com/ColetteToach

 Follow me on Twitter:
https://twitter.com/ColetteToach

 Find my books on Amazon:
www.amazon.com/author/colettetoach

 Listen to our NextGen Prophets Podcast on Spotify

RECOMMENDATIONS BY THE AUTHOR

The Apostolic Handbook

The Apostolic Handbook is the most detailed resource on the decisions you need to make in your apostolic call. I don't believe you'll find a guide more dedicated to making your journey clear and actionable.

Apostle Colette Toach is one of the church's experts in five-fold ministry leadership. She is known for simplifying the too-often mystified ministry roles into easy-to-follow guides. Here, she builds your knowledge of necessary functions in the apostolic. This includes mentorship, spiritual parenting, apostolic vision, and leadership. Illuminate your dark path with this enlightened teaching.

The Apostolic Handbook will reshape how you view your obedience to God and train you to think in a way that expands the kingdom of heaven daily. Achieve success that lasts and honor your Heavenly Father with a life that produces enduring results. Lead God's people with confidence and clarity.

You find *The Apostolic Handbook* on amazon.com.

Recommendations

Confront the hurts of the past to unlock your true prophetic call. We all have reactions that stand in the way of our prophetic ministry. Things that overpower our emotions, twist our thoughts, and force us to make decisions we regret. Where do these reactions come from, and how do we get rid of them so they no longer hinder us?

Prophetic Boot Camp

In Prophetic Boot Camp, Apostle Colette Toach takes you through the part of prophetic training that requires you to look at the pain of your childhood. You'll face the relationships you had with your parents, the negative experiences that shaped you, and you'll go through deep inner healing.

All of this is necessary to achieve the identity of a healed, powerful prophet. God wants to replace your pain with His full acceptance. In this book, you will learn:

- ⇨ Why you had to go through what you did and how God plans to use it today
- ⇨ How to put sin and flesh to death so you can experience life
- ⇨ Why you react badly to certain people, situations, and circumstances, and how to change your response to honor God
- ⇨ How to go through and minister healing to Christians
- ⇨ The 3 phases of prophetic training and which phase you're in today
- ⇨ The importance of prophetic mentorship

Prophetic training starts with healing. Start your training today!

You find *Prophetic Boot Camp* on amazon.com.

TRIBE

 If after reading this book you've decided you want champion training, prophetic peers to sharpen your sword with, and work with an apostle, join our TRIBE at [my-prophetictribe.com](myprophetictribe.com)

You'll find your place amongst an elite group of prophets who train to build the kingdom of heaven effectively. They'll be your battle buddies and teach you the power of peer relationships. With weekly webinars, a vault of teachings, and private training sessions with Apostles Craig and Colette Toach, you'll dominate the battlefield.

Being part of this tribe means you never face the battlefield of life alone. Your uniqueness is celebrated as we help you identify your ministry and the leader you're meant to work with. You'll help believers experience a face-to-face relationship with Jesus. You'll see broken hearts healed, demons bound, and relationships restored. You'll do all of this through re-parenting, mentorship, training, impartation, deliverance, inner healing, and teaching of the Word.

Join your TRIBE at myprophetictribe.com

REFERENCES AND CITATIONS

CHAPTER 1:

[1] Augusta Raurica, Bildungs-, Kultur- und Sportdirektion des Kanton Basel-Landschaft (n.d.). *The Roman City of Augusta Raurica in Basel, Switzerland,* accessed August 3, 2023 https://www.augustaraurica.ch/en

[2] Dictionary.com, LLC (2023). *Word search: alliance,* accessed August 3, 2023, https://www.dictionary.com/browse/alliance

[3] Dictionary.com, LLC (2023). *Word search: align,* accessed August 3, 2023, https://www.dictionary.com/browse/align

[4] See Acts 15

[5] See Acts 16

CHAPTER 2:

[6] Merriam-Webster, Incorporated (2023). *Word search: corps, accessed August 4, 2023*, https://www.merriam-webster.com/dictionary/corps

CHAPTER 3

[7] James Strong, A Concise Dictionary of the Words in the Greek Testament and The Hebrew Bible (Bellingham, WA: Logos Bible Software, 2009), "Submission"

CHAPTER 4

[8] Kingdom Encounters International (2018), accessed August 4, 2023, https://calebwampler.com/

[9] Hammond, Frank & Hammond, Ida Mae (1990). *Pigs in the Parlor. The Practical Guide to Deliverance.* Kirkwood, Missouri: Impact Christian Books

CHAPTER 5

[10] Japan Experience (2016). *Samurai Sword Making, accessed August 3, 2023,* https://www.japan-experience.com/plan-your-trip/to-know/understanding-japan/samurai-sword#:~:text=%22It%20often%20takes%20a%20whole,firing%20it%20in%20the%20tatara.

[11] Sword Ecyclopedia (2022). *Broadswords: Their Types and History,* accessed August 3, 2023, https://swordencyclopedia.com/broadswords/

CHAPTER 6

[12] Ancient Pages (2023). *Curtana – Sword Of Mercy Once Belonged To The Anglo-Saxon King Edward The Confessor And Perhaps Even The Arthurian Hero Tristan*, accessed August 3, 2023, https://www.ancientpages.com/2017/07/16/curtana-sword-mercy-belonged-anglo-saxon-king-edward-confessor-perhaps-even-arthurian-hero-tristan/)

CHAPTER 9

[13] See 1 Corinthians 9:19-23

CHAPTER 10

[14] See 2 Samuel 3:26

CHAPTER 14

[15] James Strong, A Concise Dictionary of the Words in the Greek Testament and The Hebrew Bible (Bellingham, WA: Logos Bible Software, 2009), 75.

[16] Dictionary.com, LLC (2023). *Word search: rebuff,* accessed August 3, https://www.dictionary.com/browse/rebuff

[17] James Strong, A Concise Dictionary of the Words in the Greek Testament and The Hebrew Bible (Bellingham, WA: Logos Bible Software, 2009), "Valiant/Valor"

CHAPTER 15

[18] Swanton, Justin (2020). *Ancient Battle Formations.* Barnsley, England: Pen and Sword Books

CHAPTER 16

[19] www.roman-britain.co.uk (n.d.). *Roman Centurions,* accessed August 3, 2023, https://www.roman-britain.co.uk/military/centurions-in-ceasars-army/

[20] See Matthew 8:9

CHAPTER 17

[21] Judson, Harry Pratt (2011). *Caesar's Army: The Evolution, Composition, Tactics, Equipment & Battles of the Roman Army.* Publisher: Leonaur

www.ingramcontent.com/pod-product-compliance
Lightning Source LLC
Chambersburg PA
CBHW070948180426
43194CB00041B/1744